M000209339

To Dearest Liz

# Underground Cathedrals

## Mark Patrick Hederman OSB

on your birthday

21 May 2010

with all my love

Mark

the columba press

First published in 2010 by
ᴄhe ᴄoᴌuᴍʙᴀ pʀess
55A Spruce Avenue, Stillorgan Industrial Park,
Blackrock, Co Dublin


Cover by Bill Bolger
Photograph of the author by Fanny Howe
Origination by The Columba Press
Printed in Ireland by ColourBooks Ltd, Dublin

ISBN 978 1 85607 695-1

# Contents

*In memory of five spiritual pioneers*
*all named John*
*who died between 2006 and 2008;*

*and in celebration of three persons*
*who will have revealed to us by 2010*
*the sound of God*
*the trace of God*
*and the mysteries of God*

# Introduction

*The Truth of Poetry*

In its beginning
The truth of poetry is a light,
Sheltered,
Vulnerable,
Awaited,
Yet no mere spark of a moment,
Exhausted,
Ephemeral.

Sufficient to make a promise,
At times undelivered,
Unaccompanied, its glow fades,
Insufficient for the making
Of such a fire,
As truth demands.

And thus from bog-beginnings moulded,
Gleaned out of history,
No longer curatorial,
Is torn from time's tomb of decay,
Of dying and transforming life,
A necessary companion,
In fire alliance.

The turf chosen for utility,
With labour, sweat and stealth,
In combination,
Is called to share again,
The task of crafting,

Making a new promise,
Offering a temporary truth.

The truth of poetry flickers
As the fire takes.
Truthmaking feeds the flames,
That blaze again,
Become beautiful in the light,
And in the fire is seen,
For a moment,
Possibility
Unquenchable,
Transformed,
Reborn out of time,
Out of decay,
As the flames rise.
And sparks soar,
Before the turf expires.

Nor yet is this an answer.
Such fire as truth requires must draw
From a source inexhaustible.
Such fire as will make of hope,
A possibility made inevitable,
Awaits the lighting.

The courage stoking,
The shared joy,
And struggle too,
For what is possible,
Release demands,
Exhilaration,
Unpredictable,
An act of faith,
And witness too,
The return in time,
To ashes unavoidable
Marks no simple defeat,
Of hope or desperate prayer.

To ask that for a while,
The fire might last,
Indomitable,
Unquenchable,
Offer in its flames a promise,
Such as truth requires of poetry,
An illusion as might suffice
To face another day,
In expectation,
Is how we make our prayer.

Then let us pray,
For those who hope,
That from the raking of the ashes,
And the placing of the seed,
For a new fire,
And a new day,
In eternal renewal,
Such a fire may come,
As offers that light,
As lets them see,
Even for a while,
The fragile truth of poetry,
Revealed,
Enough for the going on.

*Michael D Higgins*
*3 February 2009*

Why should I believe that I can somehow explain what has happened to the people of Ireland as we pass into the second decade of the twenty-first century? Why should I want even to try to articulate what I think? The answer to the first question is that I have led a privileged life through the second half of the twentieth century and happened to be in various strategic places at decisive times, not as a player on the pitch, but as a stowaway watching from a peephole, and seemingly placed there as one who might later describe the scene for those coming afterwards. The answer to the second question is linked to the word 'philosophy.' I have sometimes seen myself referred to as a philosopher and I have always refused such a description. Even though I have studied philosophy and taught it for many years, I believe that the title 'philosopher' should be attributed only to that handful of thinkers in each century whose originality and comprehensive overview of the human situation secures them a place in the history of 'philosophy'.

The study of philosophy and 'having a philosophical disposition' are different versions of the same disease. They involve being condemned to meaning, 'having to find out,' having to articulate a satisfactory explanation for whatever is going on or whatever has happened. If you wake up one morning and throw back the blinds to find that the world outside is a completely different place from the one you closed the curtains on yesterday, you don't just accept this change as 'given' and get on with it, you are compelled to discover the connection between what you see before you now, posturing as the only kind of world available, and what was there the day before.

Add to this the third element of difference, and the answer is complete. I am a monk, and the task of a monk is to contemplate the meaning of this world from the point of view of God. This happens through the agency of God's ever-present Spirit, who is guiding the world, with all the discretion and tact necessary, because the driving-seat has been definitively handed over to us, as free creatures, to lead it where we will. And 'where we will' is very often neither in its best interests, nor in ours. And yet, in spite of all that, the hovering Spirit, who has been brooding over the chaotic waters since the beginning of time, is searching out landing space, lifeboats, lighthouses, where this same Spirit can infiltrate, can put the counter-cultural plan in train, so that eventually the divine safety operation for the planet will succeed. Monks are like secret agents, with poor radio equipment, trying to maintain contact with headquarters and receiving signals about where the next move of the Spirit has been, or will be, made.

We are living in spiritually destitute times. The institutional church, which was for many a bastion of dogmatic truth, of divinely appointed moral law, of sure and certain guidance towards the heaven we looked forward to, has been discredited in the short space of about thirty years, as the new century turned its course. How did this happen, and to whom or to where do we now turn?

The Holy Spirit does not rely on the institutional church exclusively; the church of God is made up of so many more people than comprise its hierarchy; God's prophets are to be found everywhere and anywhere in the world. During the twentieth century a great rift occurred between church authority and artists in many different fields. However, many of those who were condemned by the church were, in fact, acting as secret agents for the Holy Spirit. They were constructing an underground cathedral where the true God might be worshipped, in spirit and in truth, by people in touch with the whole of their humanity.

Ireland in the twentieth century witnessed a bifurcation of the two charisms which constitute the church of God. On the one hand, there was a claustrophobic attempt to defend the orthodoxy of the apostolic principle, as this is incarnated in the hierarchy and the episcopacy. In Ireland an episcoparchy was established, in collusion with the newly elected government of this country, which turned it into something of a police state. The authoritarian guidelines for such moral and social totalitarianism were provided by the Catholic Church and specifically by the Archbishop of Dublin from 1940 to 1972, John Charles McQuaid. He maintained the orthodoxy of divinity as he understood it. On the other hand, the prophetic principle, which inspires those who are on the watch for the God who comes, rather than the God who has already spoken, had to be defended in such restrictive and claustrophobic circumstances by those who challenged the totalitarianism of the first principle, in the name of humanity. These protesters insisted that the full picture had not yet been painted; that there was more to twentieth-century humanity, the person on whose behalf God had come into the world to redeem, than the Irish Catholic hierarchy had ever dreamed of. And these artists were determined to exercise their charism, in defence of the orthodoxy of this humanity, in face of opposition and persecution from the upholders of Catholic doctrine. It was their courage and integrity which kept alive the other essential principle of Catholic truth, the work of the Holy

Spirit, who inspires the prophets of each century to speak the word of God as it emerges newly and freshly in every age. One such prophet was John McGahern, whose 'Love of the World' was second only to God's, 'who so loved the world that he gave his one and only Son, that whoever believes in him shall not perish but have eternal life.'[1] This was the title chosen for the collected essays of McGahern published posthumously in 2009. The phrase was borrowed from Hannah Arendt and was the title of one of McGahern's last short stories. His writing, as Stanley van der Ziel, the editor of these essays and writings, describes: 'with its constant savouring of every meticulously observed detail, like the ideal act of literary criticism he envisaged, is always an act of love.'[2]

There is a kind of reading done by monks which is similarly an act of love. It is called *Lectio Divina* or 'spiritual reading'. It is reading as rumination in the way a cow might chew the cud: slow, attentive but dispassionate assimilation of a text. Such reading is usually directed towards the Bible, theological or spiritual texts. But it can also be exercised on works of art and literature in a reading of 'the signs of the times'. These 'signs of the times' are the ways in which the Holy Spirit of God manifests God's creative presence in our world. To achieve this presence it is necessary to find human co-operation; such collaboration is most usefully and fruitfully accomplished through co-option of an artist. The work of such artists contains the hallmark of the Spirit and can be authenticated by detection of the indelible watermark inscribed in the results of such co-authorship. The work of art itself is the enduring evidence which remains. The artist involved need not necessarily be aware of the unseen co-operation of the hidden Spirit, but this does not mean that such synergy has not taken place. In the depths of the unconscious where great art evolves, the various hidden influences are not always transparent to the one who is chosen to crystallise it in a work of whatever kind. Far from believing that a blueprint of the world and of human nature has already been provided and is definitively in the possession of a particular institution or

1. John 3:16.
2. John McGahern, *Love of the World*, essays edited by Stanley van der Ziel, Faber and Faber, London, 2009, p xlii.

magisterium, the artist knows that 'we grow into an understanding of the world gradually. Much of what we come to
know is far from comforting ... but even that knowledge is
power and all understanding is joy, even in the face of dread,
and cannot be taken from us until everything is. We grow into a
love of the world, a love that is all the more precious and
poignant because the great glory of which we are but a particle
is lost almost as soon as it is gathered.'[3]

Such art can be as powerful a modifier of human being as
genetic engineering. The direction in which it points could be
more aligned with what we should be, more appropriate to
what we are, because it is grounded in the truth of being. A certain kind of thinking is necessary to prepare art for its essential
task and to prepare us for awareness of its achievement. The
growth and the shedding of cultural skin which determine the
movement of human history are a combination of thinking and
art, with art playing the original role. Art has the imagination to
sketch out the possible. When this happens something entirely
new comes into the world. Often it is not recognised for what it
is and is rejected or vilified by those who are comfortable with
what is already there and afraid of whatever might unsettle the
*status quo*. Someone has to stand between the new work of art
and the people who receive it, acting as interpreter.

Monks have the job of connecting things which otherwise
seem allergic to one another. This is one of the tasks of contemplation. Monks also have the task of pointing out places where
God has been identified, and where ceremonies of thanksgiving
to God have taken place.

I feel like one of those in this country who was astride the
divide, and in a privileged position to survey what was happening here during the twentieth century, almost as though I were
placed there to chronicle what happened before, during and afterwards. But, I believe that I have a very big responsibility to
defend God, Father, Son and Holy Spirit, in all of this. What has
happened was in no way their doing, all these institutions, all
these aberrations were the work of human hands. There is God,
and there always has been God, and there is always the possibility of being in touch with God, wherever we are and whatever

3. John McGahern, *Memoir*, London: Faber and Faber, 2005, p 36.

our circumstances. I have no brief whatever for the Catholic Church in Ireland in the twentieth century. I abhor and detest the inhuman institutions which were created to deal with the 'unwanted' children of our so-called 'pure' and 'unadulterated' vision of ourselves as a society. My heart goes out to each and every one of the unfortunate children who were condemned to such inhuman institutions.

What I am saying is this: those who ran these institutions were also victims of a wider and deeper conspiracy. Now is an opportunity to look at these realities with more wisdom and circumspection. To achieve this goal I have always pleaded for a deep listening to the voice of the artist in our midst, and also to the supreme artist who tries to lead us to completion, the Holy Spirit of God.

I have not tried to undertake a comprehensive survey of artistic endeavour in the twentieth century. I have simply allowed the Holy Spirit to point out to me, often in strange and unconventional ways, certain works of art which have been carriers of that same Spirit. These works remain as monuments on the landscape and by seeing them from a certain perspective, and observing the way in which they interconnect, it is possible to trace an outline which in its turn can contribute to the architectural plans for the new cathedral which we need to construct if our worship in the future is to be wholesome and life-giving. The first part of this book is a survey of where we have come from, the reasons why the old cathedrals we were accustomed to use can no longer house our religious aspirations; the second will introduce certain Irish artists, in many different art forms, who have sketched out for us during the twentieth century possibilities for an alternative and more satisfactory architecture for the future.

CHAPTER ONE

## *Overground Cathedrals*

We belong to a biological species which is now, for better or for worse, definitively in charge on this planet. *Homo Sapiens*, as we have been taught to label our species, has been on earth perhaps 50,000 years. It was not a foregone conclusion that our unlikely species, out of the millions of others, would eventually gain hegemony. In the race for the survival of the fittest, the bookies in the Mesozoic era would hardly have given you great odds on this puny little creature making it to the finishing line. Dinosaurs, gorillas, cheetahs and pterodactyls must surely have been favourites long before 'Comply or Die,' which was the motto of our particular team, as well as our winning strategy. Those of us who have seen films such as *Jurassic Park* will be aware of what it was like to live in a world where other species were in charge and where we were like irrelevant insects crushed between claw and hoof. It took us, with a great deal of evolutionary effort, 100,000 years to produce the first billion of our species; now, in this blessed twenty-first century, we are producing a billion every ten to fifteen years. We have subjugated the other species and are not just in charge, but here to stay.

As human beings we are, more or less, programmed by our nature to devise for ourselves a satisfying explanation of the universe into which we were thrown. We are not like plants which are rooted in 'one dear perpetual place' opening themselves naturally to the influence of the sun. Nor are we like insects that are active and restless, it is true, but, at the same time, totally absorbed in their daily routine. Such creatures are naturally connected to their socio-economic order. They are at home in the universe.

We are different. We are not 'at home' in the world. We are the least equipped of all the inhabitants of our planet and the most restless. The fact of being born into a world for which we are unsuited makes us frustrated creatures. This frustration defines us – we are metaphysical animals. We are physically rooted on the planet but our aspirations are elsewhere. 'Meta' means beyond in Greek; so, 'metaphysical' means 'beyond the physical.' We cannot believe (except for 2½% of us) that there is nothing more. Over 90% of the 7 billion people on the planet believe that there must be a world elsewhere.

Reason is the effect of such tragic circumstances, not their cause. Reason is secondary. It helps to describe the way in which we come to terms with our being-in-the-world. Reason is the only instrument which allows us to deal with an otherwise impossible situation. We think, only because we have to. We have no other way of pitting our inadequacy against the odds which surround us. Every one of us begins with the question: 'Why am I here?' Our existence, unlike the other species on the planet, is a question-mark. This question-mark haunts us and makes our lives an insecurity, a search for meaning. The great philosophers of history are those who have coherently posed the question to themselves. They have not only formulated the question satisfactorily but they have tried to provide adequate answers. Their answers become a system which can embrace every aspect of every life. To have one's answers recorded in the history of philosophy, it is not enough to provide a personal remedy for personal problems. Philosophy must ensure that what is proposed as the ultimate meaning of life can be shown as incontrovertibly certain and universally applicable.

The history of such thinking in our European situation goes back to Greece, about twenty-six centuries ago. Before that time our ancestors were totally engaged in the struggle for survival and had little time left over to engage with the significance of such survival. It was only when a fairly secure framework of life had been established, which allowed leisure to ponder, a certain breathing-space from the constant fear of attack and the threat of annihilation, that they could afford to ask themselves why they had bothered to struggle for survival in the first place. And so the first Western European philosophers appeared on the scene. They worked away at the meaning of the world around them and eventually produced a 'worldview' which helped to establish 'civilisation' as we know it and as we began to record it as history.

Since then, there have only been about three significant attempts to reformulate the basic design of life which we inherited from the Greeks. Three times in twenty-seven centuries, an average of once every nine hundred years, is not a lot. Perhaps this is owing to a conspiracy between the lazy conservatism which is our nature, and the powerfully convincing system left to us by the Greeks. All our philosophy, over twenty-seven centuries, amounts to footnotes to Plato and Aristotle, you might say. Many philosophers have said it before you. But the empire that took over from the Greeks and made Greek culture a worldwide phenomenon was Rome. What we call the Graeco-Roman world is the one we have inherited in Europe as our essential patrimony. And 'patrimony' is the word!

*Homo Sapiens*, is made up, fortunately, of two kinds: male and female, although the title chosen for this double act might not suggest the better half. This division between male and female does not simply occur between men and women, it occurs in differing degrees within the biology of each and every one of us. It is a question of one chromosome as to whether you appear as Bernard or Bernadette, David or Goliath, Joseph or Josephine. But it makes a huge difference to your welcome to our world.

We keep on hearing of ancient civilisations, including our Celtic forbears, who were not male chauvinist pigs but had a balanced and egalitarian attitude towards women; we sometimes hear, mostly about the pre-history of far-of islands in the Pacific, that women ruled the roost and instead of patriarchal domination you had matrilineal administration. I don't believe much of it, and experts in various fields of ethnology have described such discoveries as romantic projection of idealised scenarios upon nonexistent or indecipherable evidence. Whether it is true or not seems impossible to prove or disprove definitively, and for my argument here, accurate depiction of prehistoric societies is not essential to the case. The facts, unfortunately, seem to point towards universal domination, from the beginning, of the bully boys in the school yard of our species, at least in the known history of the universe. Men have always dominated and masculinity has at all times and in all places usurped the feminine. Certainly, the patriarchal society of the last two-to-four-thousand years, with its excess of male power and energy, has been responsible for many of the world's present problems: ruthless pursuit of power, destructive exploitation of the natural world, nuclear weapons, violence between nations, denigration of women, child abuse, racial oppression, unbridled competitiveness, untrammelled materialism.

This universal human tendency to eliminate where possible the feminine principle has radically impoverished ourselves and our planet. We have only recently been made aware of a tendency in our humanity towards genocide which the twentieth century made so flagrantly transparent that we had to do something about it. So we did what we could, setting up international tribunals to punish the perpetrators etc; but we have not yet been made fully aware of the tendency towards 'gynecide'[4] which is the universal attempt to purge ourselves and our planet of the feminine principle.

The human species, who have taken over this planet comparatively recently, in terms of its overall history, is afflicted by 'gynecidal' tendencies. These tendencies are based upon denial of the womb in order to flatter male narcissism and give us the impression of invulnerability and immortality. Once we have defined ourselves as spiritual beings striving for perfection but encased within a fleshly body, it follows that our destiny is to fight for transcendence of this body and realisation of our immortal self. Woman was defined as essentially a creature of the flesh and a threat to the transcendent powers and aspirations of the man. Woman is designed in a way that prevents her from harbouring the delusions of immortality which it is possible for a man to preserve even as he enters his ninetieth year.

Child-bearing, menstrual cycles, breast-feeding are ever-present ungainsayable reminders of the fleshly and temporal inevitabilities of our bodily make-up. These are not inscribed in the male version of the species and this allows that version to sublimate them and create an illusion of everlastingness. The fact that a man can remain sexually potent until he expires of old age allows him to indulge his fantasy of omnipotence beyond anything that a woman would be likely to entertain. However, it

---

4. 'Gynecide' is an invented term, equivalent to 'genocide' where the 'race' to be wiped out are the women of the species! ['gyne' in Greek = woman + 'cide' from Latin 'caedere' = to kill].

means that the man has to obliterate all the evidence of mortality which surrounds him and unfortunately the chief witness to such 'weakness', the incarnation of all his trembling fears of blood and guts reality, is the woman standing in front of him. So, feminine – as in 'ethnic' – cleansing removes the problem, provides the ultimate solution. Get rid of the 'woman' and immortality spreads out before you uncontaminated. This is what allowed the French philosopher, Lachelier to wake up one morning at the age of 26 and say: 'This morning I have made a remarkable discovery: I am the son of a man and a woman; that disappoints me, I thought I was a little more than that.' No woman could have taken so long to make such a 'discovery'.

Such delusionary and lethal penchants threaten not only the women of our populations but the entire principle of femininity which pervades the species as a whole. This war against the feminine principle is destructive of art and therefore of our future. Art is essentially, like all new birth, a work of the feminine principle. Art is also the only way to sketch out the future as this future should be, and must be, if we are to survive as human beings. Art alone is imaginative enough to describe a brave new world where seven billion people can cohabit and thrive.

Art, as W. B. Yeats knew, is made 'by what is still blind and dumb within ourselves'. The enlargement of experience which makes us capable of the truth of Being 'does not come from those oratorical thinkers, or from those decisive rhythms that move large numbers of men and women, but from writers that seem by contrast as feminine as the soul when it explores in Blake's picture the recesses of the grave, carrying its faint lamp trembling and astonished.'[5]

The gynecydal tendency of our species has produced, not only worldwide sexism, which we are beginning to redress slowly but surely, but violent, sometimes maniacal, hatred for, and extirpation of, any manifestation of the feminine inside the male variety itself. What is important in our society today is to begin to understand and recognise that there is a huge variety of gender, infinite and complicated permutations of both the male and the female, in each one of us as human beings. Sexual identity, even in men, ranges from the ultra-masculine ape-man at

5. W. B. Yeats, *Essays and Introductions* (London, 1961) pp 317-8.

one end of the spectrum to the zillion transsexual zebras at the
other, and until we begin as a society to understand and to celebrate this kaleidoscope of possibility in every new human being
we bring into this world, we are likely to provide them with a
straitjacket too narrow to wear. In all our societies today, all
over the world, there is an ever-increasing number of persons in
physical bodies which contradict their socially determined gender
group.

If ultra-male 'men' are in charge, if their psychology is taken
as essentially and biologically 'masculine' and normative, then
it is no wonder that women are appalled by the statistic that
only 12% of those working in the higher echelons of computer
technology are women. What kind of monsters are the male
psyche likely to produce and what kind of world are they likely
to usher in for our children?

People of the ultra-masculine variety, whether male or female,
do not ask themselves questions about the likely results or consequences of their investigations and experiments; they concern
themselves simply with what can be achieved, with what com-
binations can be elucidated, with the furthest horizons of our
inventive powers. Such uncontrolled and irresponsible craving
for novelty, at the control board of the most advanced technological capacity to create virtually anything we decide to create,
should give us pause.

One of the reasons why philosophy is incapable of showing
us the way forward at this time is because it has been, from its
beginning, a Western European all-male preserve. Henry Higgins
is representative of 'the philosopher' from Aristotle to
Wittgenstein when he describes women in general:

Why can't a woman be more like a man?
Men are so honest, so thoroughly square;
Eternally noble, historic'ly fair;
Who, when you win, will always give your back a pat.
Well, why can't a woman be like that?
Why does ev'ryone do what the others do?
Can't a woman learn to use her head?
Why do they do ev'rything their mothers do?
Why don't they grow up – well, like their father instead?

Mrs Pearce, you're a woman ...
Why can't a woman be more like a man?
One man in a million may shout a bit.
Now and then there's one with slight defects;
One, perhaps, whose truthfulness you doubt a bit.
But by and large we are a marvellous sex!
Why is thinking something women never do?
Why is logic never even tried?
Straight'ning up their hair is all they ever do.
Why don't they straighten up the mess that's inside?[6]

'Why is logic never even tried?' Because, says Iris Murdoch, it is totally incapable of 'straightening up the mess that's inside'. And the mess is what we *are*, what we *all* are, as human beings, on the inside.

Iris Murdoch studied philosophy at Cambridge and was professor of philosophy at Oxford university for over fifteen years. In that role she undertook a subversive and revolutionary guerrilla warfare against the subject she was supposed to be professing, which left Heidegger's so-called elision of all that history between Parmenides and himself in the halfpenny place. She studied all the great philosophers from Plato to Wittgenstein. She seems to have come to the conclusion that philosophy is a game invented and played by men. It is supposed to answer all the fundamental questions about human existence but fails to do so, mostly because it is too cerebral, too abstract, too scientific, too generalised. Her fundamental intuition is that life in its human manifestation is unique, unpredictable, uncategorisable and messy. Trying to capture it and freeze-frame its essence, as a butterfly collector might display specimens in a cabinet, is a waste of energy. The mystery of human existence is too mercurial and elusive to be trapped in any butterfly net, however fine the mesh. 'Human lives are essentially not to be summed up, but to be known, as they are lived, in many curious partial and inarticulate ways.'[7]

So, she abandons 'the game' of philosophy and decides in-

6. Alan Jay Learner, *My Fair Lady*, Penguin, 1960, pp 113-5.
7. Letter to David Hicks, January, 1943, quoted in Peter J. Conradi, *Iris Murdoch, A Life*, London: HarperCollins, 2001, p 529.

stead to write novels which would capture and unfold certain aspects of the human predicament. Her first, when she was thirty-five in 1954 was called *Under the Net*, as if to convey the depths into which she had to dive in order to examine the reality which lies below and beyond the nets (a favourite image of Wittgenstein)[8] laid out by the hunters and trappers in the history of philosophy who have tried for over two centuries, at least in the Western-European tradition, to stalk and capture this same prey.

Its advantages and its strengths in terms of clarity, precision and muscularity of thought, are the very reasons why it becomes powerless in the realms of Being. This is not just because the heart has reasons which reason cannot know, as Pascal has said, but because our understanding is wider than the narrow compass of our reasoning.

---

8. Wittgenstein's *Tractatus*, 6, 341, for instance.

CHAPTER TWO

## *Romanesque & Gothic Architecture*

The history of Christianity in Europe spans twenty-one centuries. This is a tiny period in terms of the age of the planet. It can be seen as the history of one lifetime if we give each century the significance of one year in the life of one person. Using this reduced spreadsheet we can describe this present moment today, in the twenty-first century, as reaching our majority. We are twenty-one, we have become adults. Looking back over the centuries of our childhood and adolescence, in this same miniature perspective, we can see how Western Europe, as it emerged, until the age of sixteen, was dominated by the powerful thought of two influential people, Augustine of Hippo and Thomas Aquinas. They, in their turn, relied heavily on the two great geniuses of Greek Philosophy, Plato and Aristotle. We can attribute to each of these, responsibility for the two dominant architectures which created our worldview from the age of six to the age of sixteen. Architecture in this sense is a symbol of the way in which we construct a satisfactory house for ourselves to live in.[1] The first kind of shelter was the Romanesque, which was an adaptation and appropriation of Roman architecture, and the second was the Gothic, a further development of this same Graeco-Roman template.

Augustine was born in 354 in North Africa at Tagaste, in modern Algeria. From the age of nineteen until he was twenty-eight he belonged to the Manichaean religion which developed from Persia where Mani (born around 216) developed a philosophy based upon the belief that there were two independent first principles of being, one good and the other evil, and that life was a constant struggle between these two principles. This essential dualism of life manifested itself within the human per-

1. I have borrowed this image and this way of presenting the history of Western Philosophy, with a few variations, from Martin Buber, *Between Man and Man*, Macmillan, New York, 1964.

son, in a conflict between the soul and the body, which mirrored
the eternal warfare in the cosmos. In this struggle our flesh, our
bodies, our sexuality were encompassed by the evil principle
which was constantly pitted against principle of the good,
which was spiritual, intellectual, immaterial. Such a division is
perfectly understandable but it created an entirely false dichotomy
which has marred our Western European landscape ever since.

At the time which concerns us here, the Emperor Valentinian
appointed a very gifted civil servant called Ambrose to the office of consular governor of Liguria and Æmilia, with residence
in Milan. In the late 300s, there had been a deep rift in the city of
Milan between Catholics and Arians. Reconstructing the life
and teachings of Arius is problematic. None of his original writings remain in existence. The emperor Constantine ordered
their burning while Arius was still living, and any that survived
were later destroyed. Those which have survived are quoted in
the works of churchmen who denounced him as a heretic, leading us to question their reliability. Whatever about the actual
position held by Arius, the basis of his disagreement with others
in the church was his refusal to see Jesus Christ as equal to the
Father. The Second Person of the Trinity was somehow created
by the Father. His views caused major controversy in Christendom at the time, unleashing the greatest theological and political conflict the church had yet known, presumably because it
was the first major doctrinal confrontation after the legalisation
of Christianity by the Emperor Constantine.

Ambrose, therefore, had to go to the church where the election of a new bishop was to take place in Milan. The previous
bishop had been Arian in tendency, and the governor had to be
present to prevent a battle between supporters of both sides of
this divide. Ambrose's preliminary address to the people re-
questing calm and dignity was interrupted by a call for
'Ambrose as bishop!' which was then taken up by the whole assembly. Ambrose was known to be Catholic in belief, although
not yet baptised, but he was also acceptable to Arians because of
the fairness and consideration he had shown in his dealings
with them. At first he fled to a friend's home and energetically
refused the office being foisted on him. He was in no way prepared for such an office; nor had he any formal training in theol-

ogy. When his host received a letter from the Emperor endorsing the people's choice, he gave Ambrose up to the people.
Within a week, Ambrose was baptised, ordained and installed
as Bishop of Milan. As bishop, he adopted an ascetic lifestyle
and apportioned his money to the poor. He gave away all his
land, making provision for his sister, Marcellina, who later became a nun. Using his excellent knowledge of Greek, which was
then rare in the West, he studied the Hebrew Bible and Greek
authors. He applied this knowledge as a gifted preacher, concentrating especially on exegesis of the Old Testament. In 384,
while teaching rhetoric as a brilliant young philosopher in
Milan, Augustine heard Ambrose preaching and then began to
read the works of the Neoplatonists. Augustine, who up to then
had thought poorly of Christian preachers, was converted to
Christianity in 386, impressed by Ambrose's rhetorical ability.
In an interesting and revealing quotation from his *Confessions*,
Augustine shows the influence which Ambrose's personality
had on his own conversion to Christianity: 'Ambrose himself I
esteemed a happy man, as the world counted happiness, because great personages held him in honour. Only his celibacy
appeared to me a painful burden.'[2]

In a famous passage in his *Confessions*, a bestseller from that
time to this day, and still available in paperback, Augustine was
standing in his garden when a voice came to him saying *'Tolle et
lege'* ('take and read') with reference to the Bible.[3] Augustine

2. Augustine, *Confessions*, Book Six, Chapter Three.
3. I cast myself down I know not how, under a certain fig-tree, giving
full vent to my tears; and the floods of mine eyes gushed out an acceptable sacrifice to Thee. And, not indeed in these words, yet to this purpose, spake I much unto Thee: and Thou, O Lord, how long? How long,
Lord, wilt Thou be angry for ever? Remember not our former iniquities,
for I felt that I was held by them. I sent up these sorrowful words: How
long, how long, to-morrow, and tomorrow? Why not now? Why not is
there this hour an end to my uncleanness?
So was I speaking and weeping in the most bitter contrition of my heart,
when, lo! I heard from a neighbouring house a voice, as of boy or girl, I
know not, chanting, and oft repeating, 'Take up and read; Take up and
read.' Instantly, my countenance altered, I began to think most intently
whether children were wont in any kind of play to sing such words: nor
could I remember ever to have heard the like. So checking the torrent of
my tears, I arose; interpreting it to be no other than a command from

having converted to Christianity in 386 was baptised a year later. He returned to Africa in 388 and sold his property to live as a monk. He was ordained priest in 391, and five years later, in 396, was Bishop of Hippo.

Although St Thomas Aquinas admits that Augustine was 'permeated by the doctrine of the Platonists' he claims that 'anything in their writings which he found consistent with the faith, he adopted; and whatever he found contrary to the faith he amended.'[4] In a more recent study Joseph Stephen O'Leary has pointed out some differences between the God who spoke to Augustine in the garden and the God who became the subject of his major writings in *De Trinitate* and *De Civitate Dei*.[5] In a very short period after his conversion to Christianity this very brilliant man was required to provide for the whole of Christendom, at a time of huge turmoil and disruption, a satisfactory and comprehensive synthesis of Christian theology. It is inevitable that elements and structures from other sources should have crept in to cover the huge surface of the cathedral he was trying to erect so speedily. Even he was aware of some of these shortcomings. He spent a year before his death at the age of seventy-six, in 430, trying to correct various errors he was aware he had made, enumerating these in his *Retractationes*.

From our point of view, it is his teaching on marriage and

---

God to open the book, and read the first chapter I should find. For I had heard of Antony, that coming in during the reading of the Gospel, he received the admonition, as if what was being read was spoken to him: Go, sell all that thou hast, and give to the poor, and thou shalt have treasure in heaven, and come and follow me: and by such oracle he was forthwith converted unto Thee. Eagerly then I returned to the place where Alypius was sitting; for there had I laid the volume of the Apostle when I arose thence. I seized, opened, and in silence read that section on which my eyes first fell: Not in rioting and drunkenness, not in chambering and wantonness, not in strife and envying; but put ye on the Lord Jesus Christ, and make not provision for the flesh, in concupiscence. No further would I read; nor needed I: for instantly at the end of this sentence, by a light as it were of serenity infused into my heart, all the darkness of doubt vanished away.
*The Confessions of Saint Augustine*, Book VIII, Paragraphs 28 and 29.
4. *Summa Theologiae*, I, 84,5.
5. Joseph S. O'Leary, *Questioning Back, The Overcoming of Metaphysics in Christian Tradition*, Seabury, New York, 1985.

sexuality which seems especially deficient. The Manichees placed sexuality in the realm of evil and it became one of those forces against which we were required to struggle for our life-time. Augustine saw the act of sexual intercourse as a direct result of original sin. As humanity sinned against God in the person of Adam, so our sexual urges are the resultant punish-ments for that original sin. This view was made even more ex-plicit by John Chrysostom (347-407) who held that 'only after the banishment from paradise did the question of sex arise. Adam and Eve lost their virginity once they became disobedient. Before that, children were born through God's creative act, since our first parents had the nature of angels.' This identification of our spiritual nature with the angelic state was one of the root causes of the duality which has plagued us since then.

Intercourse had to be for the purpose of procreation if it were to be free from sin. Catholic views on sexuality have been influ-enced by Augustine's negative approach and his 'glorification of the celibate state'. Augustine 'believed that there was nothing rational, spiritual or sacramental in the act of intercourse.' He saw it as intimately linked to original sin, a distortion that has blighted Catholic theology until the present day. Augustine says quite bluntly that sex is corrupting if it is enjoyed, and in fact a man who loves his wife with passion is an adulterer. This negative, if not abhorrent, view of sexuality is incompatible with the Christianity as taught, for instance by the great mystics, but it re-emerges even in the 1994 *Catechism of the Catholic Church* where marriage is once again described in language 'straight out of Augustine'. These last quotations come from Seán Fagan[6] who has spent a lifetime pointing out the defects in our moral theology, especially in the area of sexuality.

---

6. Seán Fagan, 'The Abuse and our Bad Theology,' *Responding to the Ryan Report*, ed. Tony Flannery, Columba Press, Dublin, 2009, pp 14-24. Here is Fagan's own account of his ministry: Ordained in 1953, I have been teaching moral theology (as well as philosophy, scripture and some canon law) in Dublin since 1955. At intervals since 1960 I have taught moral theology and spirituality to international renewal groups of priests, nuns and brothers in Europe, Asia, Africa and North America. For the past fifty-one years I have heard confessions and given spiritual direction in twelve countries of widely different lang-uages and culture. What I most remember from all of this is the enormity

Sexuality, in such a framework, became identified with evil. To say that there can be no expression of sexual energy outside the married state is to condemn all other sexual energy to paralysis or lawlessness. On the other hand, and more importantly for the argument here, is the elevation of virginity to the highest pinnacle of the perfect life. For St Thomas, and the teaching of the Catholic Church, 'perpetual continence is required for perfect piety'[7] and that is why Jovinian was condemned as a heretic because he tried to put 'marriage on the same level as virginity'.[8] The first cathedral was designed for angels and everyone seemed happy to pretend that this was quite appropriate.

If we describe the first convincing house that was built for us in the Christian era as a temple built in the Romanesque style of architecture, which has its corresponding thought-pattern in the writings of St Augustine, then we can say that human beings in Europe seem to have inhabited that temple fairly contentedly for many centuries. Romanesque architecture could be described

---

of the harm done to Catholics by what we now realise was the spiritual abuse practised unknowingly by the church for centuries. After several hours in the confessional on a Saturday night (with penitents who confessed weekly or monthly) I often came out on the verge of tears, thinking: what in God's name have we done with people's consciences? One of the great blessings of my life was that I seem to have missed the fear and scrupulosity that marked the lives of so many people, both growing up and into adult years. From infancy my God was the loving God of infinite compassion, who smiled on his creation, one who did not have to close his eyes or turn his back when I took a bath or discovered that I was a sexual being convinced that the female human body is the most beautiful of all God's wonderful creations. I sat through many hell-fire sermons and retreats and listened to all the warnings, but they never bothered me seriously, although they reminded me that I could mess up my life and hurt people by not keeping close to God. Hell fire was certainly in the background, but I never thought that large numbers of people, if indeed anybody, would be punished in that way. Even as a teenager, when I read of saints who spoke of souls dropping into hell like leaves in wintry weather, I was annoyed, but I simply felt that one could be a canonisable saint and still talk nonsense.

7. 'Utrum perpetua continentia requiratur ad perfectionem religionis' S.T. II-II, 186, q 5 art. 4.

8. 'Continentia perpetua requiritur ad perfectionem religionis, sicut et voluntaria paupertas. Unde sicut damnatus est . . . Iovinianus qui adequavit matrimonium virginitati.' S.T. II-II, 186, 4, c.

as the first pan-European style since the buildings of imperial Rome. The principles and explanations of life that lay at the base of this architecture were sufficient to stave off the insecurity and thirst for meaning which prompted us to question the way of life handed down to us by our forbears. So, for many centuries to come there were no really creative movements of thought in Europe. Even the Renaissance was, as its name implies, a rebirth of Graeco-Roman principles to underpin every aspect of European life in the sixteenth century. All efforts of thought and originality were geared towards the task of strengthening and preserving the Temple we had inherited from the founding fathers of the Graeco-Roman world.

The course of history itself provided the stimulus towards alternative explanations for the universe. The fall of the Roman Empire brought with it the destruction of the Graeco-Roman architecture as an adequate solution to the problem of existence. The winds of change and the chaos of destruction exposed us, once again, to insecurity and to the basic questions imposed by life and its fragility. We no longer basked in the security and comfort of a city state within a structured empire. Only two possibilities were open to us: either we rebuild the security of the lost architecture or we set about constructing another house which would provide permanent security for the future. The solution of return to the old architecture was impossible: the world had become larger and more unwieldy. We had discovered other lands and other realities which Greek philosophy had never dreamed of. Also, the arrival of God on earth, belief in Christianity as a dominant thought-pattern in Europe, had changed the playing field definitively. Another building would have to be provided. It would have to be more vast, more far-reaching, and constructed on firmer, less naïve foundations.

The second great attempt to provide security and meaning was the architecture of the Middle Ages, symbolised by the Gothic Cathedral, mirrored in the intellectual cathedral of St Thomas Aquinas. He was born in 1224 and died at the age of forty-nine in 1274. It is interesting to note that he was twice condemned during his lifetime in 1270 and in 1277, by the same Bishop of Paris, Etienne Tempier, who claimed that God's absolute power transcended any principles of logic that Aristotle

might provide. Fifty years after his death, Thomas was pronounced a saint and in 1879 Pope Leo XIII made his theology the
definitive exposition of Catholic doctrine. He directed the clergy
to take the teachings of Aquinas as the basis of their theological
positions. Even Thomas himself was unhappy about such infallibility being accorded to his work. While he was working in
Naples on the third part of the *Summa Theologiae* in December
1273, he unexpectedly abandoned his routine and refused to
dictate to his secretary. When Reginald begged him to get back
to work, Aquinas replied: 'Reginald, I cannot, because all that I
have written seems like straw to me' (*mihi videtur ut palea*). What
triggered Aquinas' repudiation of his own achievement is believed to be some kind of spiritual experience which caused him
to doubt the efficacy of logic and reason to understand God.
Nevertheless Leo XIII decreed that all Catholic seminaries and
universities must teach Aquinas' doctrines, and where Aquinas
did not speak on a topic, the teachers were 'urged to teach con-
clusions that were reconcilable with his thinking'. Theological
applications were being made to psychology and science, for
instance, to ensure that pace was being kept with the contemporary world.

Dante in his *Divine Comedy* sees the glorified spirit of
Aquinas in the Heaven of the Sun with the other great exem-
plars of religious wisdom, and at the Council of Trent, the
*Summa Theologiae* of Aquinas was placed on the altar alongside
the Bible and the decretals. In 1880, Aquinas was declared patron
of all Catholic educational establishments. The 1917 *Code of
Canon Law* presented Thomas as *the* teacher of philosophy and
theology.[9]

This *Summa Theologiae* of St Thomas Aquinas, therefore,
came to be the definitive Catholic map of the world. His philosophy exerted enormous influence on subsequent Christian
theology, especially within the Roman Catholic Church, but also
extending to Western philosophy in general, where he stands as a
vehicle, although with modification, of Aristotelianism, which he
fused with the thought of Augustine. His most important and
enduring work is his *Summa Theologiae*, where he expounds his
systematic theology resembling a medieval Gothic cathedral.

9. cf *CIC* 589, 1366.

This medieval dwelling embraced the reality of the whole universe and everything in it. It reached out towards the heavens through its soaring spire, and it contained within itself a map of all the different and varied levels of being which formed a harmonious ladder between God and the lowest level of creation. This second architectural agglomeration provided adequate housing for all of Europe for over a thousand years. The world, outside the one we were living in, was called heaven, purgatory and hell. The poets and philosophers and artists of medieval Europe supplied its geography and architecture with graphic precision. Dante described it in poetic detail. Real people lived in this building with resignation and in relative peace and security. They hardly ever asked themselves further questions about meaning or reality. Even to ask such questions seemed a blasphemy towards the God who was the author and the answer, and who had provided the very plans of this cathedral.

So much of church teaching which we have had passed down to us through our adoption of Graeco-Roman philosophy has little to do with divine revelation. Throughout the tradition of Judeo-Christianity, as with most other philosophies, there has been a negative attitude to women and all things feminine, which does not come from any divine revelation but which muscles in on natural tendency. Religious rites, for instance, connected with the 'churching' of women were not there to celebrate the birth of a child but rather to cleanse the woman from impurity which automatically accrued because of the natural way we all have of entering the world. Women's role in producing children, according to the high principled 'fathers' of the early church, had to be derived from 'the fall,' which caused our expulsion from the garden of Eden, and was therefore tainted with evil. From the sixth to the sixteenth century, women were dissuaded from taking communion during their periods.

Ritual impurity was connected to the superstition that if women touched anything during menstruation decay would follow: crops would wither, fruit rot, iron rust. Everything would lose its immortality and be reduced to dust and ashes in the presence of such human fragility. Blood was the stain of mortality. Sexuality was the debased version of everlasting life; it meant continuation as a human chain rather than fully fledged perpetuity of each one of us. As the church became institutionalised its attempt to control and extirpate all such visible reminders of mortality became enshrined in sanctions and taboos against sexuality in its every manifestation. To maintain the illusion of male immortality, it was also necessary to show that women were an inferior version of the essentially more durable male version of the species. Christianity took from Aristotle the reason for such inferiority, which derives from a defect. 'Women are defective by nature' because they cannot produce semen which contains a full human being. 'A woman is, as it were, an infertile male.'[10] When a man and a woman have intercourse, the man supplies the substance of a human being (the soul, i.e. the form); the woman provides only the matter. A fundamental principle for Aristotle is that, of the two factors or components in every being, 'form' is superior to 'matter'. Sexual reproduction demanded that the one who gives the 'form' (the male) be separate from the one who supplies the 'matter' (the female). In this way the 'lower' is not mingled with the 'higher' in the same individual. This means also, according to Aristotle, that the man rightly takes charge of the woman, because he commands superior intelligence. Such domination will, of course, benefit the women who depend, as it does various categories of tame animal.[11]

All this reasoning is probably very ingenious for the time of its concoction, but in the light of recent discoveries it becomes ludicrous. The reason for its perpetuation was that Aristotle became something of an unquestionable authority in the Middle Ages. He was The Philosopher, almost as an oracle, whose every teaching was afforded an infallibility way beyond its merits. Succeeding philosophers and theologians were slow to question his reasoning. Aristotle's views on women were therefore adopted by Thomas Aquinas, who had no real reason to question them. Like his contemporaries, he lacked scientific information on what constitutes the difference between men and women, but apart from that, he had other and, in his view, far more important problems on his mind. He devotes a whole question in the first part of his *Summa Theologiae* to 'The

10. Aristotle, *Generation of Animals*, I, 728a.
11. Ibid. I, 82f.

Production of the Woman.' Here he takes as revealed truth the Genesis story and the fashioning of Eve from the rib of Adam. After that he relies on Aristotle and Augustine for the philosophy of how all this took place biologically. He thinks that the rib was the most appropriate portion of the male body for creating the woman because a portion of the head would have given her ideas above her station, when she was destined to be controlled by the man; whereas the feet would have made her too subservient; so the middle way is the most fitting as it signifies 'social union' and it prefigures the sacramental emergence of the church from the body of Christ on the cross.[12] Should woman have been created in the beginning? Yes, replies Aquinas. But only to help man in the work of procreation.[13]

> The image of God, in its principal signification, namely the intellectual nature, is found both in man and in woman. Hence after the words, 'To the image of God He created him,' it is added, 'Male and female He created them' (Gen 1:27). Moreover it is said 'them' in the plural, as Augustine (Gen. ad lit. iii, 22) remarks, lest it should be thought that both sexes were united in one individual. But in a secondary sense the image of God is found in man, and not in woman: for man is the beginning and end of woman; as God is the beginning and end of every creature. So when the Apostle had said that 'man is the image and glory of God, but woman is the glory of man,' he adds his reason: 'For man is not of woman, but woman of man; and man was not created for woman, but woman for man.'[14]

Foetuses develop their full potential, their maleness, if they amass a decisive surplus of 'heat' or 'vital spirit' in the early stages in the womb. Females are the result of insufficient heat being absorbed by the foetus. What could have been a full man, then turns out to be a woman. Thomas continues: 'A female is deficient and unintentionally caused. For the active power of the semen always seeks to produce a thing completely like itself, something male. So if a female is produced, this must be because

---

12. *ST* I, 92. 3.
13. Ia. 92.1.
14. *Summa Theologiae* I, qu. 93, art. 4 ad 1.

the semen is weak or because the material (provided by the mother) is unsuitable, or because of the action of some external factor such as the winds from the south which make the atmosphere humid.'[15] Thomas saw woman's deficiency confirmed in her inferior intellectual powers. Living in a state of subjection to man, woman is not fully in the image of God, as every man is. The only real question for St Thomas is whether or not women needed to be created at all. This he answers with condescending reassurance in the affirmative; but he insists that even before the fall they would have been governed by men for their own good because, of course, the power of rational discernment in men is stronger by nature.[16] Women seldom 'keep a firm grip on things,'[17] and must be especially sober since 'they are not tough enough to withstand their longings.'[18]

15. *Dicendum quod per respectum ad naturam particularem femina est aliquid deficiens et occasionatum. Quia virtus active quae est in semine maris, intended producere sibi simile perfectum secundum masculinum sexum; sed quod femina generetur, hoc est propter virtutis activae debilitatem, vel propter aliquam materiae indispositionem, vel etiam propter aliquam transmutationem ab extrinseco, puta a ventis australibus, qui sunt humidi, ut dicitur in libro De Gen. Anim. Sed per comparationem ad naturam universalem femina non est aliquid occasionatum, sed est de intentione naturae ad opus generationis ordinate. Intentio autem naturae universalis depended ex Deo, qui est universalis auctor naturae. Et ideo instituendo naturam, non solum marem, sed etiam feminam produxit.* ST I, 92, 1, ad 1.
16. Ia. 92. I ad I and 3.
17. 2a 2ae. 156. 1 ad 1.
18. 2a2ae. 149.4.

CHAPTER THREE

## *Making Assurance Doubly Sure*

To preserve this whole second architecture intact, the Catholic Church developed a security system which would ring the alarm whenever dissenters or subversives appeared on the horizon. As soon as these alarm bells sounded, the culprits were rounded up and submitted to rigorous investigation and, where necessary, disposed of. In a cathedral where the authorities were in possession of absolute and divinely revealed truth, error had no rights and was eliminated perfunctorily. The Inquisition, a Latin term meaning investigation or inquest, was a legal procedure that involved the assemblage of evidence and the prosecution of a criminal trial for treason against Truth. The Dominicans, who were skilled and highly trained theologians, and who could therefore fairly adjudicate in such matters, were put in charge of this Inquisition. Suspected heretics were arrested, interrogated, and tried; the use of torture was approved by Pope Innocent IV in 1232. The Spanish Inquisition was authorised by Pope Sixtus IV in 1478; the pope later tried to limit its powers but was opposed by the Spanish crown. The *auto-da-fé*, the public ceremony at which sentences were pronounced, and victims executed, was an elaborate celebration, and the grand inquisitor Tomás de Torquemada was responsible for burning about 2,000 heretics at the stake. The Spanish Inquisition was not entirely suppressed until the early nineteenth century.

This infamous Inquisition has become a caricature of the Catholic Church at its worst. No one would today defend, and almost everyone would repudiate in the name of humanity, such methods and procedures. However, it is interesting to note that originally the Inquisition was begun for humanitarian reasons which are understandable when explained. Its intention was to prevent the injustice of mob hysteria and lynch law which spread like a plague all over Europe. The fear of witchcraft, for instance, and of 'sacral' religious powers of one kind or other, produced a reign of terror whereby anyone who was even mentioned as a witch was mobbed and lynched without trial. People could further their careers, appropriate lands, wreak revenge and settle scores, by falsely accusing neighbours or enemies of being witches or wizards, and the unfortunate victims were cruelly tortured and murdered.

It was to counteract such unsupervised lynch law that the church introduced a tribunal which would give some objective recourse to those accused of heresy of whatever kind. The later aberrations and abominations of the 'inquisition' should not distort the fact that it was begun to offset an evil even greater than it later became in itself.

When the institutional church felt itself threatened by what it perceived as the schism of the Protestant Reformation, Pope Paul III (Pope from 1534 to 1549) established a system of tribunals, administered by the 'Supreme Sacred Congregation of the Universal Inquisition', staffed by cardinals and other church officials. This system would later become known as the Roman Inquisition. In 1908 Pope Pius X renamed it the 'Supreme Sacred Congregation of the Holy Office,' shortened to 'the Holy Office' in popular parlance. This in its turn became the 'Congregation for the Doctrine of the Faith' in 1965, which continues to this day. The present Pope, Benedict XVI, was Prefect of this Congregation from 25 November 1981 until his election as Pope in 2005.

Despite all these precautions, inhabitants of the Medieval Cathedral began to question its viability and to investigate other possibilities, sometimes at the risk of their lives. Discoveries of science from the sixteenth century onwards, and our introduction to realities hitherto unknown, including aspects of the planet on which we were hurtling through an ever-expanding universe, caused many to discard the second great Western-European attempt to satisfactorily explain the universe and provide adequate housing for our fearful and questioning minds. However, the majority clung relentlessly to old truths and refused to abandon the sheltering places which had served so adequately for several centuries.

CHAPTER FOUR

## Crash Bang Wallop

According to many scholars, the scientific revolution began with the publication of two works that changed the course of science. This revolution, thereby, began in 1543 and continued through to the late seventeenth century. Nicholas Copernicus' *De Revolutionibus Orbium Celestium* (On the Revolutions of the Heavenly Spheres) and *De humani corporis fabrica* (On the Structure of the Human body) by Andreas Vesalius are the works in question. These attacked the old worldview from the periphery to the epicentre. Copernicus is generally regarded as the first person to formulate a comprehensive heliocentric cosmology which over time displaced the geocentric view that the earth was at the centre of the universe. His work was so destructive of the old system that it became known as the Copernican revolution. Before long, Copernicus was famously supported by Galileo Galilei, Johannes Kepler and Isaac Newton, amongst others.

Vesalius is often referred to as the founder of modern human anatomy. He carried out dissection as the primary teaching tool, handling the actual work himself while his students clustered around the table. Hands-on direct observation was considered by him to be the only reliable resource of accurate knowledge, a huge break with medieval practice. Previously such topics had been taught primarily from reading classic texts followed by an animal dissection by a barber-surgeon, directed by the lecturer. No attempt was made to actually check the claims; these were considered unassailable. In 1541, while in Bologna, Vesalius uncovered the fact that all previous anatomical research had been based upon animal anatomy rather than human, as dissection of human bodies had been banned in ancient Rome. Bodies of executed criminals were then made available to Vesalius for dissection. He soon built up a wealth of detailed anatomical diagrams, the first accurate set to be produced. Though Vesalius' work was not the first based on actual autopsy, his highly-detailed and intricate plates, and the fact that the artists who produced it were clearly present at the dissections themselves, made his work into an instant classic. Such works and many that came after them made it impossible to maintain the claims to imperm-eability of the medieval cathedral.

From the seventeenth century onwards plans began in more progressive camps for the provision of a third great explanation of the universe. It was a period when new discoveries in astron-omy, biology, physics led to a rejection of doctrines that had prevailed from Ancient Greece throughout the Middle Ages, and laid the foundations of modern science. The century began in 1600 with the condemnation by the Roman Inquisition and the public burning as a heretic of Giordano Bruno, the Italian philosopher, mathematician and astronomer, whose ideas threatened the medieval cathedral upheld by the church. After his death he gained considerable fame; in the nineteenth and early twentieth centuries, commentators regarded him as a martyr for free thought and modern scientific ideas.

The heliocentric theory of Copernicus had a profound and negative impact on the church. Copernicus himself was careful during his life not to incur ecclesiastical wrath. For fear of censure, he delayed publication of his findings. He even dedicated, with apparent sincerity, the famous work in which he proclaims his heliocentric theory to the pope of the day. Only later, in Galileo's time, did the church condemn Copernicus's work also, when Galileo was ordered to Rome to stand trial on suspicion of heresy in 1633, 'for holding as true the false doctrine taught by some that the sun is the centre of the world'. In 1616 the Holy Office condemned Galileo's Copernican teaching as 'foolish, preposterous and heretical, because contrary to scripture'. Before the Cardinals and Inquisitors, the old man was forced to recite, while kneeling, 'I abjure, curse and detest the aforesaid errors and heresies.' He was originally to be imprisoned, how-ever, due to his advanced age (70 at the time of the trial), the sen-tence was later commuted to house arrest for the remainder of his life. His offending *Dialogue* was banned and publication of any of his works was forbidden, including any he might write in the future.

It was not until 1758 that the Catholic Church dropped the general prohibition of books advocating heliocentrism from the Index of Forbidden Books. It did not, however, explicitly rescind the decisions issued by the Inquisition in its 1633 judgement against Galileo, or lift the prohibition of publication of uncensored versions of Copernicus's *De Revolutionibus*. As a result, the precise doctrinal status of heliocentrism remained unclear. Copernicus's *De Revolutionibus* and Galileo's *Dialogue* were omitted from the edition of the Index of banned books which appeared in 1835. In 2000, Pope John Paul II issued a formal apology for all the mistakes committed by some Catholics in the last 2,000 years of the Catholic Church's history, including the trial of Galileo.

Isaac Newton (1643-1727) is considered by many to be one of the most influential people the world has ever known. Through him the Aristotelian world of book-reading philosophers was changed into a mechanical, mathematical world to be known through experimental research. Religion, superstition, and fear were to be replaced by reason and knowledge. Newton's conception of the Universe, based upon natural and rationally understandable laws, became one of the major influences on what were to become known as the Enlightenment philosophers. These were intent on clearing the ground and founding a new tradition on the ruins of medieval thought. They wanted to build a new palace of scientific thought.

Immanuel Kant [1724-1804] in his *Prolegomena to any Future Metaphysics*[1] laid out the task as it faced all these pioneering explorers of a new world. Instead of providing grandiose architectural plans of the heavens and the earth, Kant, following Descartes, began with the one reality we can actually be certain about, the situated thinking individual. Unless this lonely traveller, shining a very limited torch out into the universe, could answer four fundamental questions satisfactorily, they had no business trying to provide satisfactory accommodation for all the dwellers on the planet. The four questions were:

1)What can I know? Unless I can establish the limitations and

1. *Prolegomena to Any Future Metaphysics That Will Be Able to Present Itself as a Science*, 1783.

the extent of my own knowledge, all further attempt to establish the ultimate significance of reality is meaningless. This first question embraces that division of philosophy known as epistemology (the science of knowing) and also the articulation of a complete psychology (what we are like on the inside) with an investigation into the rules and structure of logic. Psychology tells us what our mind is like; logic tells us how it works.

2) What ought I to do? This second question follows from the first. Having established how I set about knowing, I must then find out about doing. I must work out a life-pattern which will fulfil this end. Ethics is the branch of philosophy which concerns my regulation of my life. It involves also the domains of sociology and politics, which determine the role and the rights of others within the structure of any ethical programme.

3) What may I hope? Does our vocation as a human being depend entirely upon our inherent limitations and possibilities? Could there not be other realms and realities which cannot be reduced to the limited certitude at my disposal? This third question leads us into the domain of metaphysics, and all that lies beyond the natural and physical arena.

4) What is human being? This last is the most fundamental and includes all the other questions. It is to be noted that the modality of the verbs in the four questions moves from 'can' in the first, to 'ought' in the second, through 'may' in the third, to 'is' in the last. There is a hierarchy of enquiry at the apex of which is the source and goal of all philosophy which is the domain of anthropology.

Hegel was the last person to attempt the construction of a new edifice in philosophy which might effectively shelter modern humanity and provide us with a new security. He certainly took into account all the elements of the problem laid bare by Kant, but the resulting mansion was so complicated and so enormous that it was unrecognisable as a home. Rather like those pavilions hewn out of ice which are sometimes constructed for the winter Olympics, the house of Hegel was never lived in. It was impressive and forbidding, but it did not, as did the two that preceded it, provide adequate living quarters for real people.

This 'world in which we live' (that verifiable comfortable space) changed decisively in the first decade of the twentieth century when a new understanding of the visible world emerged simultaneously in several spheres of knowledge. Einstein's theory of relativity and Planck's quantum theory in mathematics and physics demonstrated that the world as we had experienced it for over twenty centuries was only a partial, limited and distorted fragment of a larger and, for the most part, unseen reality. Time and space are difficult for us to perceive while we are caught up in them. For 1,700 years the people on this planet had a very simplified idea of space which they had learned from Aristotle and which they took for granted until Galileo and Copernicus turned this perception upside down. Up to the sixteenth century, only 400 years ago, everyone believed that the world was made up of substantial, subsistent bodies, so distributed that the stable opaque earth was the centre of a system of concentric, transparent spheres onto which all the heavenly bodies were attached as by Velcro onto a cloth. The spheres moved as spheres and thereby moved the heavenly bodies. Every body had a natural place which was geometrically locatable by the calculations of Euclid, who lived 300 years before the Christian era. There was no such thing as empty space because, as everyone learned from their cradle, 'nature abhors a vacuum'. Such clichés were our unquestioned assumptions about reality. Bodies, which were all made up of four elements: fire, air, water and earth, were naturally at rest; and if they moved they must be moved by another body. And if they are so moved, then they will automatically seek to return to their natural place. It was very simple. And, indeed, some of us prefer to remain in this cosy world even today.

For over 2,000 years we thought of time as absolute. The clock ticked in the same way for everybody and for eternity. 1915 changed all this with Einstein's theory of relativity. Time ladies and gentlemen, please. The British astronomer Sir Arthur Eddington was asked in the 1920s if he would identify himself as one of the three people in the world who could understand Einstein's relativity theories. Eddington found it difficult to identify who the third person might be. Whatever the truth of the anecdote, it shows how difficult it was for most of us to understand the world we had now inherited.

The theories of relativity show that space and time are not absolute, but relative both to the observer and to the thing being observed. Our instinct is to regard time as eternal, absolute, immutable; to believe that nothing can disturb its steady tick. In fact it is variable and ever-changing. It even has shape. It is bound up with the three dimensions of space in a further dimension called 'spacetime'. The universe is not static. It must be either expanding or contracting, not fixed and eternal. An expanding universe resolves many problems. The universe began as a geometrical point, a primeval atom, which burst into glory and has been moving apart ever since.

By the 1950s, in the middle of the last century, we were ready to celebrate the earth's birthday. Our earth had an age that most scientists could agree upon: 4,550 million years (plus or minus 70 million years). It is incredible to realise that it was only by the second half of the twentieth century that we, in Europe, began to understand the planet on which we had been standing for twenty-six centuries. The conspiracy between church and state had prevented us from seeing what was directly in front of us, by providing a comparatively simplistic alternative explanation and backing this up with ungainsayable guarantees. Guardians of this *status quo* were prepared to kill in order to preserve this worldview.

And it was not only the Roman Catholic Church who defended such theories. Archbishop Ussher (1581-1656) Church of Ireland Archbishop of Armagh and Primate of All Ireland, famously proved that the creation of the world took place on the night preceding 23 October 4004 BC. Nor was this simply benighted speculation. Ussher's chronology represented a considerable feat of literary scholarship based on the proleptic Julian Calendar (produced by extending the Julian calendar to dates preceding AD 4 when its quadrennial leap year was stabilised): it demanded great depth of learning in what was then known of ancient history, including the rise of the Persians, Greeks and Romans, as well as expertise in biblical languages and an intimate knowledge of the Bible.

At the beginning of the twentieth century, most of the powers who held sway over public opinion had lost their hold. People became entitled to adopt any cocktail of received opinion as the ideology on which to base their lives. For many, a derived form of Hegel's attempt to provide shelter to the shivering masses became the focus of at least one of the ideologies which dominated the twentieth century.

CHAPTER FIVE

## Poverty, Chastity, Obedience: Marx, Freud, Nietzsche

Who destroyed the medieval cathedral in which Europe had sheltered for a thousand years? The answer is so vast and varied that it is impossible to cover it comprehensively. But whoever they were, destroy it they did, and it is possible to give an overview of how and why. It may have collapsed from internal combustion: it was way out of date and pressures from all sides were displaying its inefficacy. One of the most influential destroyers of the Medieval Cathedral was Martin Heidegger (1889-1976). He began life by studying to be a Jesuit in Austria. He was rejected as a candidate, for reasons of health. He then decided to study for the priesthood at the Albert-Ludwig University in Freiburg. Here he first encountered the writings of Edmund Husserl, and was directed by his superiors to change his studies from theology to mathematics and philosophy.

He married Elfride Petri, in March 1917, and shortly afterwards joined the German army. After the birth of his son, Jorg, in 1919, Heidegger, in a letter to a colleague, confessed that he had decided to break with 'the dogmatic system of Catholicism'. The church, in his view, was responsible for a two thousand year amnesia perpetrated by those in charge of the medieval cathedral we have been describing. It was only through courageous apostasy that he escaped this all-pervasive institutionalised blindness. The church's power was not only historical; it was psychological, sociological, economic. The ambiguity for Heidegger was that the church was not simply the source of the oblivion which he believed it was his duty to undelete, but it also had been the source, both financially and intellectually, of his own capacity to effect this revolution. The church, as his educator and his sponsor, had provided him with the wherewithal to undermine her. He had been trained, with ecclesiastical scholarships, in and through that very theology which had sub-

46

stituted itself, in his view, for the reality it was p
preserve. The young philosopher could never have
metaphysical stature that makes him one of the gre
the twentieth century without the sustenance and ~~~~,
provided by the very institution he was now destined to destroy.
On at least three occasions his career as a recognised philosopher depended upon his openly declared allegiance to the
philosophy proposed and maintained by the Roman Catholic
Church. Such compromising preconditions to the only profes-
sional advancement available to a young man of impoverished
background forced him to be ambiguous and, at a later date, aggressively censorious.[1]

However, Heidegger's attack on the very metaphysical
structure of the medieval cathedral, devastating though it may
have proved in the long term, was as nothing to the attacks
which accumulated against its moral fabric. These were legion
but, for the purpose of representative summary, I have reduced
them to three.

Karl Marx (1818-1883) made use of Hegel's dialectical method
as a powerful weapon for the critique of established politics and
religion. 'The philosophers have only *interpreted* the world, in
various ways. The point, however, is to *change* it.' 'The reality,
which communism is creating, is precisely the true basis for
rendering it impossible that anything should exist independently
of individuals, insofar as reality is only a product of the preceding intercourse of individuals themselves.'[2] In other words,
there is no divinely inspired architecture at all. Anything we
build is the result of human planning and human organisation.
'Religion is the sigh of the oppressed creature, the heart of a
heartless world, just as it is the spirit of a spiritless situation. It is
the opium of the people. The abolition of religion as the illusory
happiness of the people is required for their real happiness. The
demand to give up the illusion about its condition is the demand to give up a condition which needs illusions.'[3] Not only

---

1. For a more extended treatment of this cf my article 'Heidegger's reading of poetry: Art as Spiritual Exploration' in Phelan, H. (ed) *Anáil Dé: The
Breath of God: Music, Ritual and Spirituality*, Veritas, Dublin, pp. 121-39.
2. Vol 1, Part 4, *The Materialist Conception of History.*
3. *Contribution to the Critique of Hegel's Philosophy of Right* (1843).

was the medieval cathedral to be abolished but its builders were also to be removed. Marx summarised his approach in the first line of chapter one of *The Communist Manifesto* published in 1848. 'When Engels and I first joined the secret Communist Society we made it a condition that everything tending to encourage superstitious belief in authority was to be removed from the statutes.'[4] Although he remained a relatively obscure figure in his own lifetime, his ideas began to exert a major influence on workers' movements shortly after his death. The idea that there could be a divinely inspired architecture for the housing of humanity was nonsense. Everything we build is built by us and every building begins in the imagination of some particular human being. If we want to change the way we live we only have to develop enough imagination to do so. 'A spider conducts operations that resemble those of a weaver, and a bee puts to shame many an architect in the construction of her cells. But what distinguishes the worst of architects from the best of bees is this, that the architect raises his structure in imagination before he erects it in reality.'[5]

His influence gained added impetus with the victory of the Marxist Bolsheviks in the Russian October Revolution of 1917. Since then, few parts of the world have remained significantly untouched by Marxist ideas in the course of the twentieth century. 'Communism differs from all previous movements in that it overturns the basis of all earlier relations of production and intercourse, and for the first time consciously treats all natural premises as the creatures of hitherto existing men, strips them of their natural character and subjugates them to the power of the united individuals. Its organisation is, therefore, essentially economic, the material production of the conditions of this unity; it turns existing conditions into conditions of unity. The reality, which communism is creating, is precisely the true basis for rendering it impossible that anything should exist independently of individuals, insofar as reality is only a product of the preceding intercourse of individuals themselves.'[6] There is nothing

---

4. 'Against Personality Cults,' from a November 10, 1877 letter to W. Blos.
5. *Das Kapital: A Critique of Political Economy*, (1867) Volume I, Chapter 7, p 198.
6. Volume I, Part 4, *The Materialist Conception of History*.

there apart from what we decide should be there; and we can create for ourselves the kind of world which we collectively decide to create. It is a wonderfully liberating idea but how destructively it can be interpreted and implemented we have learnt to our cost in the century since it was first enunciated.

The second great discovery of the twentieth century which undermined the medieval cathedral was the 'unconscious.' Europe and North America became both the time and the place of the 'discovery' of this subcontinent and the loci of the reaping of its whirlwind.

Psychology was the new science which was born in such circumstances and which forced its way into the underground. Because of the atmosphere surrounding its birth, it became a brash, self-opinionated know-all, repudiating all ancestry and belittling any challengers or competitors. It made exaggerated claims for its own omni-competence and took on all opponents aggressively. As the brood began to spawn, it was inevitable that totalitarian tendency and sibling rivalry would cause the newly established science to splinter into antagonistic denominations.

Sigmund Freud, as one of the first and perhaps most notorious pioneers, became symbol and symptom of 'psychology' as I am presenting it here in caricatured terms in its role in the early twentieth century. 'Psychoanalysis was and will always be Freud's original creation. Its discovery, exploration, investigation, and constant revision formed his life's work.' It is manifest injustice, as well as wantonly insulting, to commend psychoanalysis, still less to invoke it 'without too much of Freud'.[7] When, on his 70th birthday, Freud was hailed as the 'discoverer of the unconscious', he corrected the speaker and disclaimed the title. 'The poets and philosophers before me discovered the unconscious', he said, 'What I discovered was the scientific method by which the unconscious can be studied.' Long before Freud and his century, artists had both encountered and given expression to the unconscious, sometimes in symbolic form. *Moby Dick*, for instance, is an American parable. *Dr Jekyll and Mr Hyde* are previews of what happens when the unconscious is neglected. Ordinary people become monsters over night. The writings of the Brontes are peopled by archetypal characters from the

7. David Stafford-Clark, *What Freud Really Said*, Penguin, 1965, p 19.

unconscious. Heathcliff is a changeling from the dark side. Dostoevsky's stories were hailed as prophetic descriptions of later twentieth century history, whereas they were *Notes from the Underground* as he named them in an early novel.

Friedrich Nietzsche was a German philosopher of the late nineteenth century who challenged the foundations of Christianity and traditional morality. His views on the Medieval Cathedral in which we were supposed to be housed can be summed up in two quotations: 'One may certainly admire man as a mighty genius of construction, who succeeds in piling an infinitely complicated dome of concepts upon an unstable foundation, and, as it were, on running water. Of course, in order to be supported by such a foundation, his construction must be like one constructed of spiders' webs: delicate enough to be carried along by the waves, strong enough not to be blown apart by every wind.' And 'As a genius of construction man raises himself far above the bee in the following way: whereas the bee builds with wax that he gathers from nature, man builds with the far more delicate conceptual material which he first has to manufacture from himself.'[8]

Nietzsche believed in life, creativity, health. He cultivated the realities of the world we live in, rather than those situated in a world beyond. He was skeptical of all systems and claims to omniscience, especially with regard to the human condition: 'What do we actually know about ourselves? Are we, indeed, ever able to perceive ourselves completely, as if laid out in a lighted display case? Does nature not conceal most things from us – even concerning our own bodies – in order to confine and lock us within a proud, deceptive consciousness, aloof from the coils of the bowels, the rapid flow of the blood stream, and the

---

8. *Über Wahrheit und Lüge im außermoralischen Sinn* (in English: 'On Truth and Lies in a Nonmoral Sense', also called 'On Truth and Lie in an Extra-Moral Sense') is an (initially) unpublished work written in 1873 and published posthumously. I am using the translation from his *Complete Works Online*: http://www.davemckay.co.uk/philosophy/nietzsche/. Otherwise I am taking the translation from Walter Kaufmann's *The Portable Nietzsche*, The Viking Press, New York, 1954. For the remainder of these paragraphs dealing with Nietzsche I shall refer to this work with the page number in square brackets.

intricate quivering of the fibres! She threw away the key [44].' His view of 'truth' as expressed by the church, for instance, was bound to raise hackles: 'What then is truth? A movable host of metaphors, metonymies, and anthropomorphisms: in short, a sum of human relations which have been poetically and rhetorically intensified, transferred, and embellished, and which, after long usage, seem to a people to be fixed, canonical, and binding. That immense framework and planking of concepts to which the needy man clings his whole life long in order to preserve himself is nothing but a scaffolding and toy for the most audacious feats of the liberated intellect. Truths are illusions which we have forgotten are illusions – they are metaphors that have become worn out and have been drained of sensuous force, coins which have lost their embossing and are now considered as metal and no longer as coins.' Above all he believed in himself: 'My problems are new, my psychological horizon frighteningly comprehensive, my language bold and clear; there may well be no books written in German which are richer in ideas and more independent than mine.[9]

Central to his philosophy is the idea of 'life-affirmation,' which involves an honest questioning of all doctrines that drain life's energies, however socially prevalent those views might be. Nietzsche's works remain controversial, and there is widespread disagreement about their interpretation and significance. Part of the difficulty in interpreting him arises from the uniquely provocative style of his philosophical writing. His critiques of contemporary culture, religion, and philosophy centred on a basic question regarding the foundation of values and morality. He frequently delivered trenchant critiques of Christianity in the most offensive and blasphemous terms, given the context of nineteenth-century Europe. These aspects of Nietzsche's style run counter to traditional values in philosophical writing, and they alienated Nietzsche from the academic establishment both in his time and, to a lesser extent, today. In his view, 'All sciences are now under the obligation to prepare the ground for the future task of the philosopher, which is to solve the problem

9. Letter to Carl Fuchs, 14 December 1887, *Complete Works Online*, http://www.davemckay.co.uk/philosophy/nietzsche/.

of value, to determine the true hierarchy of values.' His notion
that 'God is dead' was supposed to have contributed significantly to the rise of atheism and his book *The Will to Power* (although culled from unpublished notebooks, and published
posthumously by his sister Elisabeth Förster-Nietzsche) was accused of influencing the philosophy of National Socialism in
Germany. It was made clear to him that, in view of the attitude
towards Christianity and the concept of God expressed in
*Zarathustra*, he had become in effect unemployable at any
German university.

It is not for nothing that these three influential philosophers
of the twentieth century, Marx, Neitzsche and Freud, defined
the essential motivation of the human being as wealth, power
and sex and proceeded to build their critiques of prevailing systems around economics, the will to power, and the libido. The
Catholic Church had recognised the radical nature of these
fundamental urges at a much earlier date and had supplied the
antidote in terms of three vows: poverty, obedience and chastity,
each one set to countermand the lure of wealth, power and sex.
But the object here was not to harness this essential energy and
redirect; it was to eliminate it completely. Blaise Pascal has famously
said: 'We are neither angels nor animals and anyone playing the
angel eventually displays the beast.'[10] A morality which legis-
lates for angels is not only unsuitable for human being but it
creates a straitjacket which stifles the life-giving energy of most
ordinary people.

The twentieth century in most countries in Europe was a blun-
dering between ideologies derived from these so-called 'modern'
thinkers. Ideologies are false futures drawn in big pictures by
those who take it upon themselves to shape our destiny. This battle
of ideologies, whereby narrow and inadequate philosophies or
sociologies were adopted by governments, or anyone with
power over others, whether in schools, institutions or indeed
families, as comprehensive templates for running our lives as
human beings, dogged the fate of most countries in Europe.
Such faulty ideologies can be seen in Russia and Germany, for
instance. Postmodernism, which came roaring through the sec-

10. *L'homme n'est ni un ange ni une bête et le malheur veut que qui veut faire
l'ange fait la bête.*

ond half of the twentieth century as a style and as a concept, was mostly characterised by distrust of theories and ideologies of whatever kind or provenance.

The Catholic Church, however, refused to follow these trends and retreated to the medieval cathedral which had housed the world for so many centuries. Even in the twentieth century, there was a revival of the philosophy and theology of St Thomas which became known as 'Neo-Thomism'. Thomism, as we have seen, had been the dominant philosophy undergirding Roman Catholic theology from the thirteenth century. It appeared to have triumphed in 1880 when Pope Leo XIII declared it to be the official philosophy of Catholic schools. However, as we have also seen, this hegemony was threatened by the increasing popularity of Kantian philosophical principles. In the twentieth century, therefore, the movement in favour of St Thomas divided into two tributaries. Transcendental Thomism, represented by Joseph Marechal, Bernard Lonergan, and Karl Rahner, as examples, adapted itself to Kantian thought. But another school, under the leadership of Etienne Gilson and Jacques Maritain, sought to recover a pure version of the teachings of Thomas Aquinas himself.

Etienne Gilson (1884-1978) studied at the Sorbonne in Paris, becoming professor there from 1921 until 1932. He then taught at the College de France from 1932 until 1951. In 1929, he founded the Pontifical Institute of Mediaeval Studies at Toronto University in Canada. He divided his academic year between the College de France and Toronto University until 1951, thereafter concentrating on Toronto until 1968. For Gilson, there have been only three great metaphysicians in history: Plato, Aristotle and Aquinas, and none of these had a philosophical system. Systematisation, in his view, meant the abolition of philosophy as such. Gilson condemned the attempts of later scholasticism to turn the thought of Aquinas into an all-embracing system of philosophy. His determination was to reappropriate for Catholicism the original unsystematisable intuitions of the angelic doctor. From the Middle Ages until the present time, there had been three great experiments for founding a system of philosophy, in his view, all of which had failed. The Medieval, the Cartesian and the Modern experiment, represented by Immanuel Kant.

The result, as Gilson saw it, was the reduction of philosophy to science. Its consequences were the green light for the most reckless social adventures which have ever before played havoc with human lives and institutions. Gilson was convinced that the revival of the philosophy of Aquinas, in its pure form, would open the way out of these danger zones.

Jacques Maritain (1882-1973) studied in Paris and Heidelberg and was a professor at the Institut Catholique in Paris from 1914 to 1940. He taught mainly in North America, at Toronto, Columbia, Chicago, and Princeton Universities from 1948 to 1960. He was French ambassador to the Vatican from 1945 to 1948, and later became a strong opponent of the Second Vatican Council and the neo-Modernist movement. Maritain was the most influential Neo-Thomist. Until 1926, he was associated with Action Française, the French royalist movement opposed to republicanism, democracy and liberal ideas. When Action Française was condemned by Pope Pius XI in 1926, Maritain began to elucidate a democracy inspired by Christian faith. Although he remained a staunch defender of the Catholic Church and scholasticism, he did not regard the Christian Middle Ages as the obligatory model of human civilisation. Rather, he was inclined to acknowledge the rights of a plurality of civilisations, all of which are guided by Divine providence, and proved his ability to expound historical and contemporary human and social problems in Thomist terms, which, in his opinion, enabled him to discover the relations between historical phenomena and the supratemporal order. The Catholic Church was acknowledged by Maritain as universal, supranational, supraracial and supratemporal. He insisted that the church is not the home of the elect but the refuge of sinners. He was as strongly opposed to Nazism as he was to Bolshevism. Any contradiction between the Christian faith and modern science is, according to Maritain, a legacy from Descartes and Newton, and would disappear whenever science stuck to its own business. He was the most militant exponent of the philosophy of Aquinas in our time.

CHAPTER SIX

# Galway Cathedral

Catholic cathedrals in Ireland are monuments to our imitative instincts and conservative distrust of artistic originality. After Catholic emancipation in 1829 when church building was once again a major industry and a dominant feature of every landscape in the country, two styles only seem to have been countenanced: the revival of either Romanesque or Gothic architecture. The latter almost exclusively took over from about the middle of the nineteenth century. A thousand churches were built in Ireland in the twentieth century. Five hundred of these were built in the forty years between the Second Vatican Council and the end of the century. Church architecture had basically been the same for a thousand years. Modernity, with its technological virtuosity and new use of materials, was ready to explore new dimensions. Vatican II emphasised the corporate dimension of liturgy which translated architecturally into integration of the assembly and the sanctuary, with the altar as primary focal point. There are examples of new church architecture from the 'poetic' settings of Liam McCormick to some of Richard Hurley's mouldings of the praying community. But, in general, church authorities remained faithful to the Middle Ages and refused to abandon medieval architecture.

It is therefore understandable that in 1949, the mid-point of the twentieth century, when the building of the cathedral in Galway was commissioned it should have been conceived in a hybrid Romanesque style. Ten years later, in 1959, the foundation stone was laid; seven years after that, in 1965, the Cathedral of Our Lady Assumed into Heaven and St Nicholas in Galway was dedicated. It was in December of this same year that the Second Vatican Council solemnly ended. Its revolutionary document *The Constitution on the Sacred Liturgy*, which rendered the shape, style, arrangement and setting of such buildings obsolete and anachronistic had been promulgated two years previously.

This building was almost an object lesson in insularity. While the whole renewal of Vatican II was on the boil in Europe, and myriad manifestations of new trends in art and architecture were emerging, not just as fashionable displays of technical virtuosity, but as genuine renewal of religious and theological awareness, the people of Galway were encouraged to erect, ironically and symbolically, on the site of a former prison, this gloomy monument in grey-green Galway limestone, to our refusal to emerge from the tomb of medieval Christianity.

It is clear from the late Bishop of Galway's instructions that for him art can be no more than decoration, an illustration of either scripture or a clearly formulated theology. Art is never an original source, a spiritual revelation, a *doing* of theology. It is also clear why this situation should have come about. Most leading painters and artists were freethinking spirits with little regard for authorities of any kind. They would never have been commissioned by those who were building cathedrals at the time. Instead bishops employed artists of little vision, prepared to plaster or paint their ideologies on obsolete buildings.

There are moments in history when a people get the chance to reinvent their country. The government in charge can summon whomsoever they consider capable of such fundamental thought and together they work out how to organise the country, how the society is to be run. Such defining moments came in America with the Declaration of Independence in 1776, in France after their Revolution in 1798, in Russia after 1917, and in Ireland during the first quarter of the twentieth century. We got our opportunity to define what we meant by human being and put that into practice in a restructured society. Unfortunately, the paradigm we came up with was so narrow and so pure that it left out a large number of our population and a vast proportion of our humanity.

The first half of the twentieth century was a battle for the 'soul' of Ireland. The Roman Catholic Church, as the century progressed, became the highest and the loudest bidder. This battle for the citadel became polarised into two camps, those defending a Gaelic nationalism and those promoting a cosmopolitan internationalism. Since most of the intelligentsia were Protestant, it turned into a war between cultures. Spokespersons from each side, like George Russell (AE) and Shaw, on the one hand, and leading politicians, who publicly vaunted, in contrast, the fact that they were not intellectuals, on the other, presented almost contrary opposite views of the architecture of the new nation-state. Shaw called for the abandonment of nationalism saying that it must be added 'to the refuse pile of superstitions'. Anyone who wanted to divide the race into 'elect Irishmen' and 'reprobate foreign devils (especially Englishmen) had better go and live on the Blaskets where he can admire himself without much disturbance'. The Irish language was going to be a way of cutting off influence from outside, according to AE, who was afraid it was being used as 'a dyke behind which every kind of parochialism could shelter'. He wanted 'world culture, world ideas, world science; otherwise Ireland would not be a nation but a parish.' He used *The Irish Statesman,* founded in 1923, as vehicle for his ideas. 'The cultural implications of the words Sinn Féin are evil', he wrote in 1925, 'We are not enough for ourselves. No race is. All learn from each other. All give to each other. We must not be afraid of world thought or world science. They will give vitality to our own nationality. If we shut the door against their entrance we shall perish intellectually, just as if we shut the door against the Gaelic we shall perish nationally.'

Others, like W. B. Yeats, set out to represent an alternative spiritual tradition. He believed that one of his tasks was to provide his country and, indeed, the world of the twentieth century, with the elements of a more vibrant religious life. He wrote in his introduction to Lady Gregory's *Gods and Fighting Men* (1904): 'Children at play, at being great and wonderful people' are the true reality of what we are and what we should become. 'Mankind as a whole had a like dream once; everybody and nobody built up the dream bit by bit and the storytellers are there to make us remember.' But the children of the twentieth century had put away these ambitions 'for one reason or another before they grow into ordinary men and women.' The poets and the artists and the storytellers are there to keep the dream of being great and wonderful alive. In his letters W. B. Yeats dated our defection, our detour from the true heritage opened for us by imagination and religion, to the seventeenth century. In 1926 he wrote to Sturge Moore that 'what Whitehead calls "the three provincial centuries" are over. Wisdom and Poetry return.' The twentieth century was meant to be the privileged time of reawakening.

The wisdom which Yeats believed to be our most precious heritage can only be expressed through poetry. The word of God can never be relayed through prose. If this means that the message is sometimes obscure, that is not because the poet is being deliberately obscurantist, it is because we are moving in a borderland area for which ordinary language is not designed. Yeats believed also that the whole person in the totality of every constituent part was needed to discover and embody such truth. There is a religion which reneges on its responsibility to discover such Truth and which becomes a search for immunity against the shocks of life. Such a fearful attempt to hide from the demands of human passion and human life is, for Yeats, a denial of the two essential mysteries of Christianity: creation and incarnation. Such an impoverished religion was the one being proposed, in Yeats's view, for the new Ireland of the twentieth century. According to Elizabeth Butler Cullingford, 'Yeats knew that his name had become a byword for paganism, anti-Catholicism, opposition to Gaelic culture, and snobbery' among his Catholic counterparts, and especially in the Catholic culture being supported and diffused by such publicity organs as *The Catholic Bulletin*.[1]

Roy Foster's biography[2] shows the persistence and depth of antagonism between Catholic Ireland, as incarnated in the newly established Free State and expressed in *The Catholic Bulletin*, and the 'New Ascendancy' which they saw as 'epitomised by people like WBY, Gogarty, Plunkett, and Russell, and entrenched in institutions such as the Royal Irish Academy, Trinity College, and the Senate.' *The Bulletin*, for instance, described the Nobel Prize which Yeats won in 1923 as 'the substantial sum provided by a deceased anti-Christian manufacturer of dynamite.' 'It is common knowledge,' this report continues, 'that the line of recipients of the Nobel prize shows that a reput-

---

1. Elizabeth Butler Cullingford, *Gender and history in Yeats's love poetry*, Cambridge, 1993, p 144.
2. R. F. Foster, *W. B. Yeats: A Life*, I: The Apprentice Mage 1865-1914, Oxford University Press, 1997; II: The Arch-Poet, 2003.

ation for Paganism in thought and word is a very considerable advantage in the sordid annual race for money, engineered, as it always is, by clubs, coteries, salons and cliques.'[3]

One of the major differences between this earlier Christianity and its later manifestations, especially in the version being institutionalised in Ireland after independence, but also in various Protestant variations, was its capacity to integrate the sexual as a sacred mystery central to all life of whatever kind. The character of Crazy Jane in Yeats's imagination represents the Old Testament of the Celtic race crying out against the bishop, representing institutionalised religion, especially its contemporary Irish Catholic variety. Sexual prudery and puritanism were major enemies in Yeats's crusade for a more integrated and wholesome Christianity.

However, the medieval version of Catholic Christianity prevailed. From the very beginning of our history as a newly formed independent twentieth century state in Ireland, our mental architecture was consciously designed and implemented. National identity was expressed in symbols representing our Celtic heritage, the Gaelic language, and the Roman Catholic religion. These received state and ecclesiastical support. The questionable authenticity of this cluster of symbols has much to do with our current problems. The effort to symbolise was too ideologically moulded around fictions, too accommodating towards an economically conservative tendency, a rural bias, an agrarian way of life. Such could hardly grip the imagination of a twenty-first century Ireland making its way onto an international stage and embracing the new world of technology.

Choosing symbols of identity is a work of the unconscious rather than the conscious mind. If such symbols are to be embraced unanimously, they must emerge from the prophetic imagination and somehow touch on ultimacy for all concerned. Ireland is not made up exclusively of Celts; its language, as well as being Gaelic, is also a rich and imaginative way of using English; its faith is not confined to the Roman Catholic Church. However, both the church and the government rallied behind the preferred cluster and were obsessed by the constant threat to

---

3. Foster, II (2003) p 256.

Catholic purity, from foreign, most especially English, influences. A moral panic swept through the newly formed Irish Free State in 1922, fuelled by Catholic sermonising. Many Irish politicians saw themselves as Catholics first and legislators second. Throughout our history in the twentieth century, it was not just the church and the state but also Catholic lay groups who led the charge. Church, state and the moral majority from the beginning of the century were vocally ubiquitous and unanimous in condemning perceived moral lapses.[4] This was at its most explicit in the hectoring sermons and blatant propaganda of *The Catholic Bulletin* and *The Catholic Mind*, organs established for the purpose of supervising the rigorous enforcement of Catholic morality.

But at an even less detectable level, magazines dating from the 1920s such as *Our Boys*, were launched for the specific purpose of conducting the 'Angelic Warfare for Maintaining the National Virtue of our Country.' This campaign was based upon twin ideologies: belief in the racial superiority of the Irish in terms of sexual morality, and a puritanical view of sex on the part of the Catholic clergy. The aim of the campaign was to shield the young from 'bad' influences, especially books and films.

This ideology won a major victory in the Censorship of Publications Act of 1929. It meant also that the connection between church and state was consolidated. John Charles McQuaid, who was Archbishop of Dublin from 1940 to 1972, is seen by his biographer John Cooney[5] as 'brooding in his Victorian Gothic mansion in Killiney,' the 'undisputed champion of Catholic supremacy,' and 'determined to reiterate the belief that Ireland was different from elsewhere when it came to sexual morality and practice.' Dr Noel Browne, with the defeat of his Mother and Child scheme in the 1950s, realised that John Charles McQuaid was the arbiter of public morality in all spheres of human behaviour in Ireland, particularly sexual conduct. He and John Charles McQuaid's biographer, John Cooney, were

4. Diarmaid Ferriter, *Occasions of Sin, Sex & Society in Modern Ireland*, Profile Books, London, 2009.
5. John Cooney, *John Charles McQuaid: Ruler of Catholic Ireland*, Dublin, 1999.

convinced that 'McQuaid was obsessed with protecting Catholic
Ireland from the evil nature of human sexuality.' In his fictional
essay *A Virgin Ireland*, Browne describes the mission statement
of what he calls McQuaid's 'Dreary Eden': 'John the Bishop
promised at the end of our lives, unsullied by the ugliness of
human sexuality, he would deliver us Irish to our heavenly
maker.'[6] Both Browne and Cooney detected in the archbishop a
symptom which often marks the perpetrators of such 'pure'
regimes: 'that he's totally obsessed with sex' himself. But the obsession is inverted. Rather than indulging in sexual practice of
whatever kind, his obsession is tracking down and stamping out
of any manifestation of sexual impurity in the country for which
he sees himself responsible. He becomes 'like Ceausescu in
Romania or any of these eastern European leaders … bringing
Ireland more and more under a kind of spiritual terrorism that is
austere, that is backward looking and which is also pretty strict
theologically.' As well as the 'imposition of a very severe code of
sexual conduct,' there is his horror of 'filthy' books which leads
to the banning of most great writers of the century, and his setting of spies to snoop on people with regard to their sexual
mores.[7]

Moral policing was required and imposed by the Catholic
hierarchy, who were worried about the multiplication of occasions of sin in many new-fangled entertainments, especially the
dance-halls. 'Company keeping under the stars of night had succeeded in too many places to the good old Irish custom of visiting, chatting and storytelling from one house to another, with
the rosary to bring all home in due time', was the view of one
archbishop in 1926. In 1927 the bishops issued a joint pastoral:
'The evil one is forever setting his snares for unwary feet. At the
moment, his traps for the innocent are chiefly the dance-hall, the
bad book, the indecent paper, the motion picture, the immodest
fashion in female dress – all of which tend to destroy the characteristic virtues of our race.' Once again the twentieth century in
all its technological manifestations and cultural fashions is pitted
against an almost racist view of Irish purity.

---

6. Quoted in John Cooney, p 277.
7. cf Ferriter, pp 338-9.

Such decrying of moral laxity was not just an Irish phenomenon. All over Europe after The Great War there was a fear of
degenerate moral behaviour. But, in Ireland, the new Republic
was particularly single-minded and fanatical about establishing
its own national dugout. John McGahern puts it succinctly:
'When I was in my 20s it did occur to me that there was something perverted about an attitude that thought that killing somebody was a minor offence compared to kissing somebody.'[8]
Ireland's defence would be a parochial network, walling out the
cosmopolitan tendencies of the rest of the world. The doors
were shut culturally and we remained imprisoned in our own
homemade cathedral. Critics of AE were perhaps justified in
questioning his naïveté. How could he hope, in the words of one
critic, 'to resist the tremendous, vulgarising power of Anglo-
American civilisation?' Anyway, his battle for cosmopolitanism
was lost. In the words of one recent historian, 'There was a naïve
popular belief that, left alone, Ireland would be a paradise.'

Ireland was beginning to govern itself politically also. In the
battle for the 'soul' of Ireland which was the first quarter of the
twentieth century, the Roman Catholic Church became the
highest and the loudest bidder. Far from adopting the philosophies sprouting everywhere in that same century, the Irish
Catholic Church built its foundation on the second great architecture derived from St Thomas Aquinas. It is significant that
most of the philosophy faculties of the National University of
Ireland were peopled by clerics who taught philosophy as if it
were being taught in a seminary. Desmond Connell, for instance, was appointed Professor of General Metaphysics at
University College Dublin in 1972 and in 1983 became Dean of
the Faculty of Philosophy and Sociology. He had little interest in
philosophy other than Thomism, and Dr Patrick Masterson was
made professor of 'Special Metaphysics' in the 1970s where he
could teach the beginnings of contemporary European philosophy to a new generation of Irish students. Desmond Connell
later became Archbishop of Dublin from 1998 to 2004, 'at a time,'
according to Diarmaid Ferriter, 'when he was the last person the

8. John McGahern, *Love of the World, Essays*, Faber, London, 2009.

church needed, precisely because he was inflexible and driven by his beliefs in absolute truths ... He and his fellow Thomists (the followers of ideas based on the writings of Aquinas) saw no room for doctrinal debate and individual conscience and regarded a metaphysics based on the writings of Aquinas as an absolute science. Connell argued that virginity is of a higher order than sexuality, and that the highest possessor of this virginity is "the consecrated virgin" – the male priest.'[9]

So, the Irish Free State in the twentieth century became an alignment of nationalist politics and the Roman Catholic Church. In 1937 the De Valera Constitution of our 'free' state, expressed this derived philosophy in no uncertain terms. In a radio broadcast to the United States on 15 June that same year, De Valera called it 'the spiritual and cultural embodiment of the Irish people' and to mark its first anniversary in 1938, he reminded us, almost as in a sermon: 'As faith without good works is dead, so must we expect our Constitution to be if we are content to leave it merely as an idle statement of principles in which we profess belief but have not the will to put into practice.'[10]

The 'angelic' formula, with its exaggerated emphasis on the 'spiritual' and a vilification of the 'physical', coupled with an overemphasis on self-contained identity as opposed to being-with-others, colours both our relationship with ourselves and with other people from our earliest years. The culture which presents us with such options also selects for us preferred heroes and saints who are solitary, celibate, rugged, ascetic. Those of us who cannot or will not embrace such ideals or follow such role models, are made to feel disappointing or second-rate.

Such unrealistic and arbitrary cultural ideals, even though they may produce, in exceptional cases, exotic awe-inspiring deeds and personalities, create a tension in most ordinary people. Neglect of, and disregard for the emotional and sexual side of ourselves and the other-oriented structure of our bodies and personalities has two inevitable consequences: we develop defence mechanisms and outer armour which allow us to survive undernourishment of our philanthropic appetites and we remain undereducated

9. Diarmaid Ferriter, *Occasions of Sin, Sex & Society in Modern Ireland*, Profile Books, London, 2009, pp 532-3.
10. Eamon De Valera's St Patrick's Day message on radio, 1938.

and illiterate in our relational capacity. Those of us who fail to become beautiful anchorites or hermits, have to stumble about the marketplace feeling insecure, guilty, awkward and angry.

Quoting Tom Inglis, Diarmaid Ferriter suggests that 'practices of chastity, humility, piety and self-denial, born of an oppressive Catholic culture, led to Irish Catholics being flat, awkward, embarrassed, shameful, guilty and communicatively incompetent about sex. Sex was only talked about in the context of the natural law of God and confined to religious discourse.'[11]

The training received, especially by those who entered religious life, was a lonely journey of self-sacrifice. The individual person gradually pared him or herself down to the quick, divesting themselves of all earthly attachments, until they eventually bled back into the soul of themselves where they could rise like a helium filled balloon to the throne of the most high. The important thing was to cut yourself off from all human affection and attachment, to kill off conscientiously any natural urges of the body so that the new kind of heavenly fuel, supernatural grace, might flow through the human infrastructure. You tried to be solitary, chaste, pure. You shunned all earthly goods and material wealth. Above all, you fought against your own taste, impulses, inclinations and will.

Education, in such circumstances, was strictly regulated and put in the hands of a centralised authority with control over the curriculum. As with most systems of education the intent was to brain-wash the population to acceptance of the received culture and accepted philosophy of the country. In such a context, women's education was separate and geared towards motherhood; the woman's role was presented in terms of 'virgin and martyr' with long-suffering impotence at a personal level being sometimes hailed as sanctity. Virtue can be mistaken in such a scenario for an incapacity to accede to any virtue whatsoever. The corresponding ideal of 'manhood' spells harsh and ascetic agressivity towards oneself and towards others. For a male to be soft or sentimental is betrayal of the cause. Displays of emotion are ridiculed and interpreted as signs of going 'soft in the head'.

The government used the 'Orders' in the Catholic Church as

11. Diarmaid Ferriter, *Occasions of Sin, Sex & Society in Modern Ireland*, Profile Books, London, 2009, p 24.

an unpaid task-force to provide an education and health service at minimum cost. Without these unpaid servants of the state the miracle of the so-called 'free education scheme' could never have happened. In 1824, for instance, 60% of school age children were not attending school in Ireland. At the beginning of the nineteenth century there were six congregations of religious women with a total of eleven convents. By the beginning of the twentieth century there were 35 congregations with 368 houses. The founders of these congregations were usually wealthy women with social status, who were struck by the socio-economic plight of the multitudes of poor who surrounded them, and wished to do something practical to improve their lot. They set up congregations for similarly high-minded women prepared to dedicate their lives to the betterment of humanity. These congregations were soon incorporated into the institutional paradigms of the Gothic Cathedral. An analysis of the effect of this syndrome on buildings by and for religious, entitled *From Sisters to Nuns, from Brothers to Monks* by Brendan McConvery, suggests:[12]

> It is difficult to assess the impact of the Gothic Revival on the shaping of religious life in the mid-nineteenth century, but its heritage would endure until Vatican II. The Gothic revival was a child of the late Romantic Movement and sought to retrieve a medieval tradition that was often deficient in its grasp of history ... This fascination with the Middle Ages was particularly striking in the use of a Gothic style of architecture in convent and church building. The Convent of Mercy, Birr, was founded in 1840, within about thirteen years of the beginning of the congregation. The convent building was designed by A. W. Pugin [whose] successors and Irish pupils such as McCarthy and George Ashlin, continued the trend of housing religious in buildings that were markedly medieval.

The newly established orders founded institutions to look after those excluded from the benefits of society. These were

---

12. Brendan McConvery CSsR, 'The Shaping of Irish Religious Life,' *Responding to the Ryan Report*, ed. Tony Flannery, Columba Press, Dublin, 2009, pp 35-36.

rapidly taken over by church administration and harnessed to government needs. Those in power then set up a socio-political system which condemned all who were excluded from its criteria of acceptability, to incarceration in such newly established institutions.

In 1828, for instance, Edmund Rice (1762-1844), the founder of the Christian Brothers, acquired a suitable site for his first school at North Richmond Street, in Dublin. He too was a comparatively wealthy person in his own right. He wanted the Archbishop of Dublin to lay the foundation stone for this school but Murray suggested that Daniel O'Connell should be the person to do so. It became one of the liberator's great monster meetings – about 100,000 people turned up. From the beginning, therefore, this movement was connected to the emergence of Ireland as a nationalist Catholic country. John McGahern puts it succinctly: 'The Christian Brothers had been set up by the Catholic hierarchy to counteract attempts by the British, under the Whig ministry of Earl Grey, to establish a non-religious system of education in Ireland. They were more nationalistic than other schools (set up against the godless English, their textbooks glorified nationalist violence in the past) and they were to provide much of the future IRA leadership.'[13]

Rice's motto was: 'Catholic and Celtic, to God and Ireland true.' He began his inspirational work of educating the poor people of Ireland at a particularly formative time in the history of the country, between the dawn of Catholic Emancipation (1829) and the beginning of the great Famine (1846). 'The Ireland of Rice's boyhood was not the romantic image of the "big house" surrounded by a mass of undifferentiated poverty, not the "penal era" of unrelenting persecution, but the age of endurance and emergence … In an age of rapid political development, ambitious Catholics were in a position to exploit the many occasions which arose.'[14]

Obviously the first recruits to his new order were adults and they must have received adequate and inspirational training from their founder. However, no one could have predicted the phenomenal growth which the fledgling organisation enjoyed.

---

13. John McGahern, *Love of the World*, Faber, London, 2009, pp 249-50.
14. Daire Keogh, *Edmund Rice* (1996) p 26.

By 1842 they were in Australia and by 1876 in New Zealand. They were sent to 12 different countries in Africa between 1950 and 1996 and to 4 countries in South America between 1948 and 1988. By the end of the twentieth century the Edmund Rice founded school system was catering for some 50,000 students with over 12,000 teachers. These orders of brothers and sisters were the ones who trained the Celtic Tiger as a cub. They established the infrastructure and the personnel of the education and health systems which we can no longer afford, since the free labour and unhireable dedication of so many unsung religious has evaporated.

To provide recruits for the rapidly developing empire of these orders, which they understood to be the work of the Holy Spirit, immediate and compelling recruitment was necessary. Incestuous and forced growth became almost inevitable. 15 year olds were culled from Christian Brothers' schools and given inadequate training to become as quickly as possible the personnel to run the expanding empire. Little appropriate formation was provided to equip them personally, or develop them spiritually, for the mammoth task that lay ahead.

These same orders also became the agency whereby all who were excluded from the definition of our perfect Christian society were 'looked after.' Once a community is persuaded that certain people are not worthy of 'care,' are beyond consideration as fellow human beings, then our natural sympathy and compassion can be switched off and the step towards regarding such people as a nuisance and then as expendable and finally as 'vermin' is within reach. This has been true in terms of certain tribes in all countries, in terms of women in most countries, in terms of children in some cultures, in terms of Jews in the Nazi perspective, in terms of itinerant communities in settled communities, and in terms of homosexuals almost universally during the twentieth century.

The Magdalen asylums, which were established in the eighteenth century to house prostitutes until they were reformed by punitive regimes, became in the twentieth century 'an indication of another enduring theme in relation to perceived sexual transgression – the collusion of state, society and religious orders in seeking to remove from public circulation perceived threats to a conservative moral order.'[15] The mind-set of the majority towards such outcasts was condemnatory. No one cared what happened to them, nobody wanted to know. If you cannot actually do away with them you can establish institutions where they are removed from your sight and 'cared for' by those appointed to this task.

Orphanages and 'workhouses' where unwanted children were sent, and Gulags and Concentration Camps, where 'dissidents' and those outside the definition of one particular 'model' of humanity were disposed of, have alarmingly similar traits. Stalin is said to have modelled the KGB on the strategies used in the seminary where he had trained to be a priest. Regimes designed to keep the inmates 'pure' and in line with the established template turned into playgrounds for sadists. Much of the violence and brutality in all such punitive institutions has an underdeveloped sexual aspect to it and betokens a complete failure to accept, educate and celebrate the essentially sexual aspect of ourselves as human beings. Once sexuality has been identified as the enemy of purity and excluded from the 'model' we establish as the norm, it becomes alienated and repressed and re-emerges in perverse alternative impulses.

The inevitable antagonism set up between guardians and inmates in any 'prison' situation brings out the most aggressive hatred between the two sides. Such 'warfare' was the resulting ambiance of the 'borstal' institutions we had created for the unwanted in our society. There have been recently recorded experiments done by psychology students who put themselves into evacuated prisons and divided themselves into 'prisoners' and 'guards' for a certain length of time. These experiments had to be discontinued because the people involved found themselves reverting to 'type' so archetypically that they were doing damage to themselves and to each other.[16]

But a second kind of injustice can now take place because we want to find certain people whom we can hold responsible for a situation which was the effective 'doing' of a whole society at a

15. Diarmaid Ferriter, *Occasions of Sin, Sex & Society in Modern Ireland*, Profile Books, London, 2009, p 16.
16. The *Stanford prison experiment* was a study of the psychological effects of becoming a prisoner or prison guard. The experiment was con-

certain time. In the present hysteria these religious orders could find themselves used as scapegoats for a second time. The first time to look after the outcasts of our society; and now to take the blame for what happened to those who were regarded as the problem children of the state at the time. Those who ran these institutions were also victims of a wider and deeper conspiracy. The religious orders who were asked to exercise this social function (effectively 'guards' of those deemed unsuitable for the normal integration into the welfare state we were constructing for ourselves) were victims also of the philosophy we had devised for ourselves to explain the world and create a home for ourselves on this island. Some of the 'brothers' and 'sisters' who were brought into these religious congregations, were adolescents themselves, 14 and 15 year olds, who were then submitted to a regime of fear and propaganda which made it difficult for them to think for themselves or achieve any kind of personal freedom or maturity. They were taught, for instance, which was also the current belief at the time, that children born out of wedlock had an innate propensity towards evil and should be treated with the utmost severity lest they lose their immortal souls.

The whole situation is much more complex and nuanced than we have been led to believe by media reporting. Media attention has been focused on the eighteen religious congregations which owned, staffed and ran the institutions where much of

---

ducted in 1971 by a team of researchers led by Psychology Professor Philip Zimbardo at Stanford University, California. Twenty-four undergraduates were selected out of 70 to play the roles of both guards and prisoners and live in a mock prison in the basement of the Stanford psychology building. Roles were assigned at random. They adapted to their roles well beyond what was expected, leading the guards to take authoritarian and even draconian measures. Two of the prisoners were upset enough by the process to quit the experiment early, and the entire experiment was abruptly stopped after only six days. Several guards became increasingly cruel as the experiment continued. Experimenters said that approximately one-third of the guards exhibited genuine sadistic tendencies. Most of the guards were upset when the experiment concluded early. The experimental process and the results remain controversial. The entire experiment was filmed, with excerpts soon made publicly available, leaving some disturbed by the resulting film. Over 30 years later, Zimbardo found renewed interest in the experiment when the Abu Ghraib torture and prisoner abuse scandal occurred.

the child abuse took place, but little effort has been made to con-
textualise their situations. Let it be said without equivocation
that wherever there is evidence that members of any religious
congregation are guilty of sexual abuse of children, especially
those in their care, and wherever they have been guilty of physical abuse of children they should be prosecuted and sentenced
according to the law. But condemnation without trial of all those
in these congregations, and of these congregations as a whole, is
unjust and unwarranted. If all these congregations are to be
censured then so too should be censured the other institutions
and agencies who put them in this situation and maintained
them there. The Irish government first of all is responsible for the
total situation. Having inherited the system of 'reformatories'
and so-called 'industrial schools' from Great Britain, it kept
these in place long after they had been abandoned in favour of
other possibilities by most other countries. Then the NSPCC, the
National Society for the Prevention of Cruelty to Children, were
some of those who rounded up the children in the first place.
Some of the Gardaí were major players, as were members of the
parish clergy, and the judiciary.[17]

The use of certain congregations of religious for such purposes
was an abuse in itself. It was pitting one institutionalised group
against another. And the 'carers' were underpaid, overworked,
badly trained, ill-prepared, inmates of their own somewhat inhuman organisations, with little spiritual, personal, psychological or educational formation to help them cope with the human
tragedy forced on their hands.

Terry Prone, one of Ireland's leading communications con-
sultants, has pointed out that history has now repeated itself
these last few years 'except that instead of innocent children
damaged by religious in whom their care has been vested, the
victims, this time around, were innocent elderly nuns and
priests and brothers and the attackers were the state, the media,
the general public – and their own.' She holds that their lack of
media savvy left them defenceless against expertly broadcast ex-

---

17. In what I have said in the above paragraph I am reiterating and en-
dorsing what Donal Dorr has written in 'Who is Responsible?',
*Responding to the Ryan Report*, ed Tony Flannery, The Columba Press,
Dublin, 2009, pp 111-121.

posé packages on TV, radio and the newspapers, so that they were 'lumped together as, if not collectively committed to perversion, brutality and money-making, at least culpable by association and shared culture.'[18] A more comprehensive and complex story needs to be told.

---

18. Terry Prone, 'Bricks on the Road to Hell', *Responding to the Ryan Report*, ed Tony Flannery, The Columba Press, Dublin 2009, pp 84-85.

CHAPTER SEVEN

## *I Spy with My Little Eye*

What Thomas Hardy says is true: 'If a way to the better there be, it exacts a full look at the worst.' The Ryan Report gives us a good look at some of the worst that has ever been in Ireland since we began. Now is an opportunity to look at these realities with more wisdom and circumspection (although I doubt if our children in fifty years time will look upon our efforts to be human with any less jaundiced an eye) and put in place more comprehensive models to provide adequately for all our citizens. We may be repeating past errors without realising it. That Brendan Smyth, the first priest in our society to have been publicly exposed as a paedophile and child molester, could tell us publicly about the kind of torture he endured in prison, where he was constantly beaten over the head with socks bulging with billiard balls, by other prisoners who regarded his crimes as beneath contempt, and qualitatively different from their own; that he had to be buried at midnight and a cement covering put over his grave in case the mob might dig it up to desecrate it; such realities say more about our society than they do about the person they are supposed to discredit or denounce. They show that we have learned little about ourselves. We have simply changed the victims but continued the system.

Anyone whom we decide is unworthy of human treatment is cast into prison where all forms of inhuman degradation, humiliation and abuse can be perpetrated without causing any of us even a flicker of remorse. Now we are aware that Brendan Smyth was not a unique and exceptional pariah, but that unconscionable numbers of our undernourished and ill-educated society were also child-abusers and that we have a considerable population of so-called 'paedophiles' on our hands. Are we simply to reverse the equation and submit these outcasts to the same kind of inhumanity which we allowed them to exercise on an earlier population of outcasts? These manifestations of brutality and abuse are once again signs of a society creating scapegoat monsters and operatic villains which only serve to distance us from the real nature of our own situation and prevent us from identifying the conniving partner and blood relation in our society who is the darker side of ourselves.

Ireland was kept in the dark about the darkness.[1] We were not the only population to have been consciously sheltered in this way by well-meaning authorities of one kind or another. But suppression of the darkness and unawareness of the unconscious, avoidance of all entrances to the underground, were helped by our being an island and by the cultural isolation which this made possible. Peter Gay, in his monumental study of *The Bourgeois Experience from Victoria to Freud*, tells us: 'The unconscious is intractable. At best, however tantalising the traces it may leave behind, it is almost illegible to the untrained observer. But, while the assignment of rendering it legible and accessible to historical inquiry is admittedly difficult, it remains a decisive truth of history – a truth the historian ignores at his peril and to his loss – that much of the past has taken place underground, silently, eloquently.'[2]

The accusation being made against bishops and religious superiors that they actually knew about the abuse that was being perpetrated by the various members of their dioceses and congregations, is neither fair nor true. Whatever the facts may now show, it is still true to say that thirty years ago no one in Ireland was aware of what we have come to understand as 'child abuse'. If we can divide this horrific reality into three categories, physical, psychological and sexual, then we have to accept that Ireland was a place, in the 1950s for instance, where physical punishment was rampant in every part of our society and was regarded as quite acceptable whether in the home, the school or in institutions for young people. The idea that such violence was abuse would only have been recognised in very unusual or extreme cases. Children who complained of being beaten at school might easily have anticipated further punishment of a

---

1. I have dealt with this aspect of our situation more specifically in *Kissing the Dark*, Veritas, Dublin, 1999.
2. Peter Gay, *The Bourgeois Experience from Victoria to Freud*, Oxford, 1984, p 13.

similar kind in the home where parents would presume automatically that if the child had been beaten at school it was good enough for them and must certainly have been deserved. Psychological abuse was unheard of at the time, as indeed was psychology itself.

The first Child Guidance Clinic was opened in Ireland in 1955 in Orwell Road in Dublin, where the first Clinical Psychologist was also appointed in that same year 1955. At this point in the middle of the twentieth century Child Psychiatry was hardly recognised in Ireland. A professor of paediatrics at the time felt that it had no place in this country, that we didn't need it, and at one of the Royal Academy of Medicine's Psychiatric Section meetings a member is recorded as saying that 'he didn't believe in psychology but did believe in smackology.'[3]

As regards the sexual abuse of children we have to recognise another very strange phenomenon: however much police documentation or other officialdom recorded the facts of such scandalous abuse in so many places around the country, it still remains an even more mysterious reality that the population as a whole was unaware of it. This is more especially true of people who were brought up in monasteries, convents or seminaries and who had no sexual experience themselves. The accusation that clergy were able to molest hundreds of vulnerable children because of a 'systemic, calculated perversion of power' that put their abusers above the law, is true not because their superiors were covering up for them but because their superiors had no idea whatever about the actual gruesome reality in which they were involved. All knowledge being passed on to such superiors was in words and reports. These bishops and superiors, except in a number of exceptional cases, were quite incapable of understanding the full impact of what they were hearing. What has been reported as 'the damning verdict on the conduct of church and secular authorities' following 'a three-year investigation into allegations of child abuse by priests in Dublin going back to the 1960s,' is an unwarranted conclusion. Such uninhibited

---

3. *Irish Families Under Stress*, Vol VII, '50 Years of Irish Child Psychiatry', edited by Prof Michael Fitzgerald, South Western Area Health Board, 2003.

scope was afforded to abusers in the Catholic Church because the people who were in charge were incapable of understanding the horrific realities which were being presented to them. It is as if they were tone deaf or colour blind precisely because of the total absence of any sexual education or experience in their own lives. And here we have to find analogies to help us understand a cultural purblindness which affected the whole country until the rude awakening which came only towards the end of the twentieth century.

Investigators who were recently given access to 60,000 previously secret church files in the Dublin diocese, accused four archbishops of Dublin of deliberately suppressing evidence of 'widespread' abuse. Archbishops John Charles McQuaid, Dermot Ryan and Kevin McNamara, who have all since died, and Cardinal Desmond Connell, who is retired, all refused to pass information to local police, the report said. Evidence was kept inside a secret vault in the archbishop's Dublin residence, with suspect clerics moved between parishes to prevent the allegations being made public. The truth is that the secret vault in which these written reports were 'suppressed' was within the psychology of the archbishops themselves. In a telling reply to a questionnaire in 1965, asking him whether the Irish Church was obsessed with sex, Archbishop McQuaid says in a draft which was never sent: 'No. There is probably a saner attitude to sex in this country than almost anywhere else. Family life is stable, women are respected, and vocations are esteemed. Sex, in the sense used here – illicit sex – is a sin and is the concern of the church.'[4]

In the ethics of the medieval cathedral all sex outside of marriage is a sin and endangers the immortal soul of the perpetrator. Categories of distinction between homosexual sex, premarital or extramarital sex, criminal sex, did not enter the Thomistic mind-set; the reality of sexual addiction or the possibility of psychological traumatisation of victims never occurred to either the bishops or the public at large until very late in the twentieth century. All such realities could all be 'called by their true names' learnt in the Catechism, 'fornication, adultery, lustful desires

4. Ferriter, p 341.

etc.' The conclusion drawn from the above draft by John Charles McQuaid, that he believed 'that sex is intrinsically sinful' does not necessarily follow. He believed that sex was for the procreation of children and that such was the purpose of marriage and that any sex, even in this context, which was enjoyed or performed simply for its own sake was sinful. So 'Sex, in the sense used here – illicit sex – [which] is a sin' is what Oliver J. Flanagan was also talking about when he famously declared that there was no sex in this country until the advent of *The Late Late Show* on RTÉ.

For their part, the Gardaí were also products of a whole medieval system. 'A number of very senior members of the Gardaí, including the Commissioner in 1960, clearly regarded priests as being outside their remit. There are some examples of Gardaí actually reporting complaints to the archdiocese instead of investigating them.' There is, if such is permitted, at least one hilarious incident in the Murphy Report, where John Charles McQuaid invites the Chief of Police to his gothic mansion to discuss homosexuality. The next we hear is an apologetic letter from the Garda Commissioner explaining why he had to forgo this invitation because of more important business. One can imagine the embarrassment such a proposed conversation would have caused the street-wise commissioner who would have had to hone his language to conform to his perception of his august listener.

One case cited in the Murphy Report (13:5) deserves examination because it shows, to my mind, the seismic gulf between three different types of 'understanding' which we fail to recognise from our later historical perspective. The first is the mind-set of 'the priest paedophile;' the second is the mindset of the bishop or the archbishop supposed to be in authority; the third is the mind-set of the compilers of the Murphy Report.

In August 1960, Archbishop McQuaid was informed that a security officer at a photographic film company in the UK had referred colour film, sent to them for developing by a certain Fr Edmondus, to Scotland Yard. Scotland Yard referred the matter to the Commissioner of the Gardaí. There is no evidence of any Garda investigation. However, Garda Commissioner Costigan met Archbishop McQuaid and, according to Archbishop

McQuaid's note of the meeting, told him that the photographic company had 'handed to Scotland Yard a colour film with label Rev [Edmondus], Childrens Hospital, Crumlin, Dublin, of which 26 transparencies were of the private parts of two small girls, aged 10 or 11 years.' The Garda Commissioner asked Archbishop McQuaid to take over the case because a priest was in question and the Gardaí 'could prove nothing'. The Commissioner told the Archbishop that he would do nothing further. Archbishop McQuaid immediately referred the case to his auxiliary bishop, Bishop Dunne. Bishop Dunne expressed the view that a crime of child sexual abuse had been committed. The next day, Archbishop McQuaid met Fr Edmondus who admitted photographing the children in sexual postures alone and in groups. These photographs were taken in Crumlin hospital. The archbishop recorded as follows: 'The children were playing about, lifting their clothes. He rebuked them. Seeing this was a chance of discovering what the genitals were like, he pretended there was no film in the camera he was carrying and photographed them in sexual postures, alone and seated together, chiefly in a way or posture that opened up the parts. He declared that he had done so, as one would take an art photo, seeing no grave sin at all and suffering no physical disturbance in himself. He was puzzled, though he had seen line drawings, as to structure and functions of the female. In questioning, I discovered that he had been reared with brothers, had never moved about socially with girls and tended to avoid them as in the hospital with the nurses. I suggested I would get (a doctor) a good Catholic to instruct him and thus end his wonderment.' Archbishop McQuaid also recorded: 'I felt that he clearly understood the nature of the sinful act involved and to send him on retreat would defame him.'

Archbishop McQuaid and Bishop Dunne then agreed that there was not an objective and subjective crime of the type envisaged in the 1922 instruction, and consequently that there was no need to refer the matter to the Holy Office in Rome. Archbishop Martin, on behalf of the archdiocese, suggested to the Commission that what Archbishop McQuaid was trying to establish was whether the subjective and objective elements of a canonical crime had been committed and that he found that no crime had been committed. The commission concluded: 'Given that these photographs were taken by deception, when a nurse was absent, given the nature of the photographs and the fact that the film was sent to the UK for development, any reasonable person would imply *mens rea* or criminal intent from the circumstances. The conclusion of the archbishop and Bishop Dunne that this was not an objective and subjective crime within the meaning of canon law is, in the Commission's view, unreasonable and contrary to common sense now and in 1960. It is totally at variance with Bishop Dunne's original opinion as recorded by Archbishop McQuaid a few days earlier. The Commission believes that Archbishop McQuaid acted as he did to avoid scandal in both Ireland and Rome and without regard to the protection of children in Crumlin hospital. Archbishop Martin accepts that the conclusion reached by Archbishop McQuaid and Bishop Dunne was wrong and that the measures taken were inadequate, but he does not agree with the Commission's conclusion that Archbishop McQuaid acted the way he did to avoid scandal both here and in Rome.'

The Commission then gives its assessment of the situation:[5]

'This case was very badly handled by Archbishop McQuaid. Archbishop McQuaid's conclusion that Fr Edmondus's actions arose merely from a 'wonderment' about the female anatomy is risible. The Commission considers there are two possible explanations for this stated view. Either Archbishop McQuaid could not deal with the fact that a priest who was in a privileged position of chaplain to a children's hospital fundamentally abused that position and sexually exploited vulnerable young children awaiting treatment, or he needed an explanation which would deal with Bishop Dunne's justifiable concern and which would also justify not reporting the matter to Rome. The Commission considers that the second explanation is the more likely one.'

Here we are dealing with three quite different ways of understanding. Archbishop McQuaid's terms of reference were to do with the sin or otherwise committed by the priest. As far as he was concerned, the children involved were nothing more

5. Murphy Report, 2010, The Commission's assessment 13.69.

than occasions of sin. It never occurred to him that they might have been psychologically damaged by the abuse which was quite obviously being perpetrated by the priest in question. The paedophile priest played upon McQuaid's arrogance and ignorance. But the compilers of the report fail to understand the ecclesiastical mindset and the cultural predisposition of the time, which imbued priesthood with such an aura of mystification and otherworldliness that it could not be associated with cold-blooded deviousness and criminal intent. Archbishop McQuaid was so convinced that he knew everything about human nature and priestly behaviour that he need only establish whether this particular person had been sexually aroused by taking such photographs to declare that no 'subjective or objective crime' had been committed. This is the mind-set which had been hard-wired into Catholic clergy since the middle ages and to dismiss it as 'risible' is to pre-empt the 'inquiry' which the Commission was appointed to undertake.

The inquiry also found that church authorities nurtured inappropriately close relations with senior police officers. But this went without saying at the time. Church authority was a force which invaded every aspect of life in Ireland at this time including the psychologies of every Catholic. Such judgement of inappropriateness on the part of the Commission fails to take account of the almost mythological status afforded to priesthood in the general psyche of Irish society. Members of the police force, families, people in charge of schools, hospitals, institutions were all hypnotised by this magic spell. The reason why they frequently ignored complaints from victims, and effectively granted priests immunity from prosecution, was because they also bought into the mythology that all priests were living the life of angels and that it was unthinkable that they would indulge in such activities.

In October 1995, when other former patients in the same hospital came forward alleging abuse, one of them said he had told his parents about the abuse at the time but was told not to be talking like that about a priest. The well-worn story of Irish road workers outside a brothel being scandalised as they see a Rabbi and a Parson going into the house of ill fame; but agreeing with one another that one of the girls must be sick when they see the

Parish Priest arrive on the doorstep, speaks a truth which is significant. The Gardaí in Ireland were no exception in this pan-
demic of sacerdolatry. As John McGahern says: 'The ordained
priest's position could not have been easy either. No matter
what their power and influence was they were at that time completely cut off from the people, both by training and their sacred
office which placed them on a supernatural plane between the
judgement seat and ordinary struggling mortals.'[6]

The inquiry, we are told, dismissed the claims of former
bishops that they did not know sex abuse was a crime. But the
more stunning reality is that no matter what was said to them or
presented to them verbally or on paper, they were incapable of
taking in the reality of what sex abuse was at all. I quote from Fr
Seán Fagan once again:

> Until the mid-80s I knew about paedophilia as a psychologi-
> cal phenomenon, and I was vaguely aware that some men
> "tampered with little boys" but, like most of the population,
> I was unaware that large numbers of people suffered child
> abuse as we know it now. It was never mentioned in confes-
> sion by either perpetrators or victims, and I think that few
> victims were able to reveal it, so one can hardly speak of a
> 'conspiracy' of silence. Most people were simply unaware of
> the abuse unless they had personal experience of it. I doubt if
> police or social workers knew much more. For centuries
> moral theologians listed the major sexual sins as: fornication,
> adultery, rape, abduction, incest, sacrilege (sex with vowed
> religious), sodomy, and bestiality. These were analysed in
> terms of what was natural and appropriate, just or unjust, but
> the age of the victim was never a factor of importance. Child
> abuse was not a special category because it was not recog-
> nised as such, and hardly anybody knew that the practice
> was so widespread, or so devastating in its consequences.
> The early sex scandals that brought shame (and criminal
> charges) to priests and religious around the world were not
> always about child abuse. But the publicity and court pro-
> ceedings in such cases encouraged victims of child abuse to
> speak out, and more people have found the courage to come

6. John McGahern, *Love of the world*, op. cit., p 142.

forward. Since then I have listened in counselling sessions to many victims and I become more and more horrified at the enormity of the harm done. Some extreme cases may be driven to suicide, but very many are emotionally and spiritually crippled for life. They can be helped by counselling, but it is a slow and painful process, and there is no guarantee of total success. Financial compensation can never make up for what the victims suffer. The church must name this evil as a special sin in a category of its own, and wherever church individuals or institutions are even slightly implicated, they must accept their responsibility and ask forgiveness.

In an article by Oliver Sacks called 'Scotoma: Forgetting and Neglect in Science,' Sacks suggests that most great scientific discoveries were made sometimes a hundred years before they eventually hit the headlines and were given recognition in the public domain. This is because the world was not yet ready for such a revelation. We were not yet able to handle it. 'The term "scotoma" (darkness, shadow) – as used by neurologists – denotes a disconnection or hiatus in perception, essentially a gap in consciousness produced by a neurological lesion. Such lesions may be at any level, from the peripheral nerves, to the sensory cortex of the brain. It is therefore extremely difficult for a patient with such a scotoma to be able to communicate what is happening. He himself, so to speak, scotomises the experience. It is equally difficult for his physician and listeners to take in what he is saying, for they, in turn, tend to scotomise what they are hearing.' Something similar was happening in this country when the official idiom of the church in terms of chastity, purity and celibacy, especially with regard to the priesthood as a national shrine, met up with an underworld of sexual depravity too monstrous to be entertained. Sacks continues his description of a parallel phenomenon in the world of science saying that: 'Even if barriers to communication are transcended no one seems to read or remember what they have written. There is a historical or cultural scotoma, a "memory hole", as Orwell would say.' He goes on: 'It is not enough to apprehend something, to "get" something, in a flash. The mind must be able to accommodate it, to retain it. The process of accommodation, of being able to create a mental space, a category with potential

connections – and the readiness to do this – is crucial in deter-
mining whether an idea or discovery will take hold and bear
fruit, or whether it will be forgotten, fade, and die without issue.
The first difficulty, the first barrier, lies in one's own mind, in allowing oneself to encounter new ideas and then to bring them
into full and stable consciousness, and to give them conceptual
form, holding them in mind even if they do not fit, or contradict
one's existing concepts, beliefs, or categories. This applies to all
new ideas, especially those which threaten the whole world
which you have constructed for yourself and for the mainte-
nance of which you are now the principal supervisor.' And Sacks
goes on to suggest that it is not simply that we are not ready yet
to receive the news which is being conveyed, he describes a
process of suppression which automatically prevents the unwanted
information from being registered. 'But "scotoma" involves
more than prematurity, it involves deletion of what was originally
perceived, a loss of knowledge, a loss of insight, a forgetting of
insights that once seemed clearly established, a regression to less
perceptive explanations. All these not only beset neurology but
are surprisingly common in all fields of science.'

In extreme cases, he concludes, scientific debate can threaten
to destroy the belief systems of one of the antagonists, and with
this, perhaps, the belief system of the entire culture. This is true
of the sexual revelations which at last our culture and our society are just about able to take on board. They threaten the belief
system of the whole country, which is why they were 'unthinkable' in the Thomistic mindset. With such people in charge there
is every scope for outrageous misdemeanour simply because
appointed authority is incapable of imagining any such possible
behaviour. Sacks offers one of the clearest examples of such
impossibility of taking on board in the realm of science, and the
potential destruction of entire systems of belief in 'the publication of *Origin of Species* in 1859, with the furious debates between
"Science" and "Religion" (embodied in the conflict between
Thomas Huxley and Bishop Wilberforce), and the violent but
pathetic rearguard actions of Agassiz, who felt his lifework, his
sense of a creator, massacred by Darwin's theory.'[7]

7. *Hidden Histories of Science*, ed Robert B. Silvers, Granta Books,
London, 1997, pp 150-63.

The four people who were Roman Catholic Archbishops of Dublin since 1940 were all high principled, scrupulous, dedicated and well-meaning men. They are not evil, underhand, monsters, deliberately protecting criminals and perverting the course of justice. They were exemplary products of a total system which was based upon inadequate understanding of what human being actually is, and in their dedication to the life-pattern laid out before them from a very early age, they became monuments to a whole society's misalignment.

What John Feeney wrote about John Charles McQuaid in 1974 still applies to him and to his three successors: 'He was a first-class bishop of the old school. If he had lived fifty years earlier or even if he had died after twenty years in office, he would have no critics worth speaking of and would hardly be remembered today except by those who had benefited from his quiet personal charity. He was a diligent, sincere and absolutely honest man who did his duty as he saw it ... By the end of his reign he personally had not changed greatly but others had ... he stood out as the personal embodiment of all that a new breed of liberals despised and were embarrassed by ... a figure of division and polarisation in a church which needed ... scapegoats for the sins of all churchmen in the era before reform.'[8]

However, to hold such stalwarts of the old regime culpable for the dysfunctional and criminal behaviour which inevitably resulted in society from such wrongheaded thinking, is yet one more way of shirking our own corporate responsibility. At the time they were in charge, these leaders were quite incapable of understanding or facing up to a reality which, if they were to take it on board, threatened their very being and the belief system of an entire culture. The Second Vatican Council, which sought to liberate a whole generation of Roman Catholics, was completely lost on prelates such as John Charles McQuaid. He returned from Rome after this council and in a famous sermon in the Pro-Cathedral in Dublin, said: 'You may have been worried by much talk of changes to come. Allow me to reassure you. No change will worry the tranquillity of your Christian lives.'[9]

6. John Feeney, *John Charles McQuaid, The Man & the Mask*, Mercier, Cork, 1974 p 79.
7. Quoted by John Cooney, *John Charles McQuaid, Ruler of Catholic Ireland*, O'Brien Press, Dublin 1999, p 371.

As John McGahern has said: 'Ireland is a peculiar society in the sense that it was a nineteenth century society up to about 1970 and then it almost bypassed the twentieth century.' What we are experiencing as we move into the second decade of the twenty-first century is the aftermath of a double earthquake. The tectonic plates have shifted and some of us are left standing on one side of the divide while others move off on the other. We are dealing with the double earthquake that happened in the 1960s with the Vatican Council and the Sexual Revolution. Every community in the Western world can be divided into those who came after these revolutions and those who came before. The gap at that point was too wide between the world we were opening and the one we were leaving behind. The moment of breakage between the two tectonic plates can be dated, in my view, to the Encyclical of Pope Paul VI, *Humanae Vitae*, which he promulgated on 25 July 1968. Subtitled 'On the Regulation of Birth,' this document re-affirms the traditional teaching of the Roman Catholic Church on abortion, contraception and other issues pertaining to human life, as well as reaffirming the Catholic Church's traditional view of marriage and marital relations. However, it was mainly because of its prohibition of all forms of artificial contraception that it became uniquely controversial.

There had been two papal committees and numerous independent experts looking into the latest advances of science and medicine in the area of artificial birth control before this encyclical appeared, and many people hoped that, in light of the recent Vatican Council II and its emphasis on collegiality rather than papal infallibility, the advice of such experts might have influenced the pope in his thinking on these matters. However, the encyclical opens with an assertion of the competency of the Church's magisterium to decide questions of morality. The question of human procreation exceeds in the view of Paul VI specific disciplines such as biology, demography, psychology or sociology.[10] The sexual act must 'retain its intrinsic relationship

---

10. *Humanae Vitae*, # 7: 'The question of human procreation, like every other question which touches human life, involves more than the limited aspects specific to such disciplines as biology, psychology, demography or sociology.'

to the procreation of human life', and the 'direct interruption of the generative process already begun' is unlawful. Every action specifically intended to prevent procreation is forbidden, except in medically necessary circumstances. It also insists that priests must spell out clearly and completely the church's teaching on marriage, and on human sexuality. The encyclical recognises that 'perhaps not everyone will easily accept this particular teaching,' but points out that the Roman Catholic Church cannot 'declare lawful what is in fact unlawful,' because she is concerned with 'safeguarding the holiness of marriage, in order to guide married life to its full human and Christian perfection.'

The reason why this particular encyclical, at this particular time, was the breaking-point between two worlds was, in my view, that it did not simply reiterate the division between sexuality within marriage, which was lawful, and all sexuality outside marriage which was sinful; it prescribed and proscribed for sexuality within the precincts of marriage itself. Here it was entering the domain of the heterosexual community who used to make up the moral majority happily supporting all prohibition of sexual behaviour outside their own protected area. On 4 October 1965, when addressing the UN General Assembly, Paul VI challenged his audience: 'You must make it possible to have enough bread for humanity's table; and not favour the artificial control of births – something irrational – to decrease the number of guests at the banquet of life.' *Time* magazine had a cartoon of the Pope addressing the UN with a barrage of microphones between himself and the audience, starting his speech on *Humanae Vitae*: 'If I've told you this joke before, stop me!'

The recent Murphy report shows that most abusers only began acting out after they were forty, and nothing was set in place to deal with such abuse until well into the 1990s. The sexual revolution meant that many religious and priests felt they had been duped. They had bought into, and sacrificed their sexuality to, false notions of human perfection. Far from being sinful and dangerous, their sexuality was one of the most beautiful gifts of humankind and they had been persuaded to sacrifice it in favour of a state which was now being questioned both psychologically and spiritually. Far from being an exalted state of being, celibacy and virginity were now perceived as stunted and futile.

Not only was it of no particular value from a spiritual point of view but it was emasculating from a human point of view.

Consecrated Religious people who had been taught that they were a step above everyone else in the kingdom of God, found out from the documents of Vatican II that they were no better than any ordinary lay person. Many left and got married. But many without any education or guidance began to explore their sexual proclivities and in the Ireland of the time they enjoyed a freedom and unencumbered rampancy which came from their own ecclesiastical immunity and the country's overall gullibility. Obviously, there must have been very many serial paedophiles who became members of religious orders and entered seminaries precisely because they would have a vast and unprotected catchment area for their sexual proclivities, but apart from these, the various reports emerging suggest a less bloody-minded calculation. Many began to molest children sexually because they were so underdeveloped and inexperienced in the area of their own sexuality that they needed the helpless and vulnerable to overcome their own inadequacy.

At this moment in the chaos which results from the news of both the Ryan and the Murphy reports, there is a great deal of lynch law, megaphone diplomacy, and mob oratory which fails to understand the complexity of all that was involved, and is meting out rough justice to many of those who are supposed to have been responsible.

CHAPTER EIGHT

## Dostoevsky and Medjugorje

'He's supposed to be the Archbishop of Canterbury! The Church of England is collapsing around his ears! And where is he? In America for two months! Writing a book about Dostoevsky!'[1] So some of his flock viewed the recent retreat of Rowan Williams to write his book *Dostoevsky: Language, Faith and Fiction*.[2] Dostoevsky laid the foundation of the underground cathedral which artists have been building since the collapse of the Middle Ages. Not only did he understand the depths of our potential depravity as human beings but he grasped the essential nature of evil and the work of the Devil in the world. 'Terrorism, child abuse, absent fathers and the fragmentation of the family, the secularisation and sexualisation of culture, the future of liberal democracy, the clash of cultures and the nature of national identity – so many of the anxieties that we think of as quintessentially features of the early twenty-first century – are pretty well omnipresent in the work of Dostoevsky [1].'

In *The Brothers Karamazov*, Dostoevsky presents us with a parable in which he imagines Christ coming back into our world to Seville in Spain at the time of the Inquisition, and being condemned to death by The Grand Inquisitor, who represents church authority. The day before his death, The Inquisitor visits Christ in his cell to tell him that the church no longer needs him. The Inquisitor explains to Jesus why his return to earth would interfere with the mission of the church. The Inquisitor frames his denunciation of Jesus around the three questions Satan asked Jesus during the Temptation in the Desert: the temptation to turn stones into bread, to cast himself from the Temple and be saved by the angels, and the temptation to rule over all the king-

1. A. N.Wilson, 'Where Rowan Williams meets Dostoevsky', *Telegraph*, 27 September, 2008
2. Rowan Williams, *Dostoevsky: Language, Faith and Fiction*, Continuum, London, 2008. For the remainder of this chapter I shall refer to this work with the page number in square brackets.

doms of the world. The Inquisitor accuses Jesus of rejecting these three temptations in favour of freedom, but he thinks that Jesus has misjudged human nature. He does not believe that the vast majority of humanity can handle the freedom which Jesus has given them. Thus, he implies that Jesus, in giving humans freedom to choose, has excluded the majority of humanity from redemption and doomed it to suffer.

The multitude then is guided through the church by the few who are strong enough to take on the burden of freedom. The Inquisitor says that under him, all humankind will live and die happily in ignorance. Though he leads them only to 'death and destruction,' they will be happy along the way. The Inquisitor will be a self-martyr, spending his life keeping choice from humanity. 'Anyone who can appease a man's conscience can take his freedom away from him.' Christ was wrong to reject each temptation of Satan. Christ should have turned stones into bread, as people will always follow those who feed their bellies. The Inquisitor recalls how Christ rejected this saying, 'Man cannot live on bread alone,' and explains to Christ: 'Feed people, and then ask of them virtue! That's what they'll write on the banner they'll raise against Thee.' Casting himself down from the temple to be caught by angels would cement his godhood in the minds of people, who would follow him forever. Rule over all the kingdoms of the earth would ensure their salvation, the Grand Inquisitor claims.

Rowan Williams sees all fascism, all attempt to remove freedom from people and replace it with dictatorship, however benevolent and inspirational, as the opposite of Christianity and the work of Satan:

> The Devil desires authorship, and the Inquisitor's world is *his* narrative. And the result is that every human being becomes a child again, and is guaranteed the 'sweetness' of childlike happiness and innocence [78].

There is a double desire at work here: that of the hierarchy in the church who lust for power and take over control of the free will of those over whom they have been put in charge; and that of the people who long for security and the strong hand of fatherhood to remove from them the anxiety and ambiguity of working out their own salvation.

The Devil is out to stop history; he is the enemy of narrative and so of the freedom of persons to shape their identity over time [93]. The Devil's desire is to spare us the complications of contingency by securing for us a protracted childhood [79].

The Roman Catholic Church in Ireland in the twentieth century tried to fulfil this role of removing from the people their freedom and responsibility for working out their own salvation, reducing them to infantilism and treating them like children. John McGahern concurs: 'I came to whatever intellectual age I am in the Dublin of the late 1950s and early 1960s. There is not the time to dwell on it here, but I believe it's not too crude to say that church and state had colluded to bring about a climate that was insular, repressive, sectarian ... A childishness in religion and politics and art was encouraged to last a whole life long ... I think it is no simplification to state that the country was being run almost exclusively for a small Catholic middle class and its church.'[3] Those who rebelled or disobeyed instructions were ostracised. However, the 'other voice' was kept alive by novelists who undertook to supply the other half of a dialogue which was never allowed to take place.

Dostoevsky works on the basis that the novelist is able to show in some degree what divine creation might be like: that is, by creating a world in which the unexpected and unscripted is continually unfolding, in which there is no imposed last word. The novelist attempts a self-emptying in respect of the characters of fiction, a degree of powerlessness in relation to them. We best read Dostoevsky as working through this analogy between writing and divine creation ... to introduce to the imagination a model of making that is directed toward freedom and not control [234].

The imposition of a regime of totalitarian control does not stem simply from the 'will to power' of the few who are in charge. It stems also from a deep-seated desire on behalf of the majority of people. We long for leadership of a convincing kind. Unconsciously we dream of a return to childhood where all the major decisions of life can be taken by some authoritative figure

3. John McGahern, *Love of the World*, op. cit., p 97.

who receives a mandate from some ungainsayable power. That is why we are so moved by news of apparitions from heaven which tell us that all is well, that we will be safe as long as we become children again and adopt a supine and credulous attitude towards a set of instructions dictated from above.

Medjugorje ('between the hills') has become well-known in Bosnia-Herzegovina, and the world, because of six young people who claim to have seen visions of the Mother of God there since 24 June 1981.

I went to Medjugorje from 23-30 June 1991 to form an opinion about the spiritual validity of the place where the Virgin Mary was supposed to have appeared to these six young visionaries and to have done so on a daily basis since that time. At first their claim was met with skepticism and hostility. The word '*mir*' (meaning 'peace') was written in the sky on 2 August 1981, in a way similar to what had happened at Fatima, and this was seen by some of the villagers. The setting sun revolved and drew nearer to the church and, in October, a large flame was seen on the mountainside where Our Lady had first appeared. These events came to the attention of the local authorities who tried to dispel all such religious fantasy. Meetings on the hill were forbidden as they amounted to political rallies in the eyes of the authorities. So, the apparitions moved to the church. In the room where they now occur, the children enter, begin praying the rosary, and suddenly fall to their knees in 'ecstasy'. This happens, they report, when the Virgin Mary is present. Their lips move as though they were engaged in conversation but there is no sound. Her departure is indicated when the visionaries say '*O De*' meaning 'She has gone.' Then they continue the rosary and leave when they have finished.

There has been no shortage of scientific experimentation to prove the authenticity or the hoax. Needles have been stuck into the visionaries in ecstasy and examination undertaken of the retinas of their eyes. Photography has documented the process in detail.

The local bishop Zanic of Mostar claimed that the whole thing was a show put on by the Franciscans to get money and power. He promised to do a pilgrimage on his knees from Mostar to Medjugorje if the apparitions were shown to be real visitations to the village by the Mother of God. Almost like a comic opera, the metropolitan archbishop of the region was Franic of Split. So, Franic and Zanic were at loggerheads and a high pitched propaganda battle was in full swing. At the time of my visit bishops and priests had been advised by the local ordinary not to organise or take part in official visits to the shrine. I was not a priest and I travelled incognito.

As recently as 29 September 2009, the Bishop of Mostar-Duvno, Ratko Perić, stated in a homily:

> Brothers and sisters, let us not act as if these 'apparitions' were recognised and worthy of faith. If, as Catholics, devoted sons and daughters of the church, we want to live according to the norms and the teaching of the church, glorifying the Holy Trinity, venerating Blessed Mary ... and professing all that the church has established in the creed, we do not turn to certain alternative 'apparitions' or 'messages' to which the church has not attributed any supernatural character.

Such episcopal prohibition seems only to promote the cause! When I arrived, there were about 200,000 people assembled for the tenth anniversary of the first apparitions. Such a figure is not accurate. However, there are official statistics of 100,000 who made the journey from abroad by plane and it is reasonable to estimate that at least this number again arrived by bus from Italy, Germany, France, Austria etc.

The village itself is situated in western Herzegovina which is mostly Croatian and Roman Catholic. It is in the centre of the country in a valley surrounded by limestone hills. Apart from the attractive mountain scenery which, I am reliably informed, is of the same ancient karst as the Burren in Co Clare in Ireland, nothing else in the area would entice the ordinary tourist. The journey is long: three hours by plane from Dublin to Dubrovnik, followed by another three hours in a bus which arrives at three o'clock in the morning.

There were no hotels specifically. This is Our Lady's village and the people preferred to receive the pilgrims as part of their family. Arrival at three in the morning was certainly a good start for testing their hospitality. The house where we were billeted seemed to have been built the day before yesterday and in some hurry. It was a rough and ready hostel like a square box with six

rooms upstairs, a kitchen and dining-room downstairs, a number of washrooms and three toilets. Two or three people slept in
each room. Two beds and a mirror on the wall completed the
furnishings of each low-ceilinged snowcem cell. Our window
overlooked a dump facing a dirty blank wall. Debris from recent
building activity was scattered all around. Landscaping was not
part of the hurried brief and such houses were being thrown up
all over the countryside.

The 'family' in our 'home' comprised three nuns (two of
whom had brought with them one other member of their own
families, in one case a brother, in the other a sister), a Tipperary
farmer with his wife and daughter, an American couple from
New Orleans, a Dublin scrap-merchant and his wife, and my
room-mate from Mayo, recently appointed assistant-manager to
Dunnes Stores in Nenagh. Our first meal was presented by
'Rosa,' the house-mother, at three in the morning and was eaten
in silence. We then had a long sleep until 9.30 am when we had
breakfast of Lyons tea (bags) and Michelstown Dairy Bawn
powdered milk, left behind by previous cosmopolitan visitors.

The village itself (most of which disappears overnight and re-
turns by seven in the morning in the shape of endless stalls and
tents, selling fruit, food, maps, post-cards and bric-à-brac, plus the
inevitable galaxy of shrine memorabilia: statues, rosary beads, pictures, plastic madonnas filled with holy water, devotional literature and prayer books in several languages), is an elaborate front
with no back. Every construction is providing some service for pilgrims. There is even a special agency for pilgrimages from Ireland.

The dearth of aesthetically pleasing objects or buildings is
highlighted by the one visit during our stay organised to
Mostar, the nearby town, built on the river Neretva which divides it with unusually green water and unites it with a series of
spectacular bridges. The Roman remains and Turkish influence
give exotic flavour to its architecture, whose most famous feature is the bridge built in 1557 (Mostar means keeper of the
bridge), which made it strategically important for trading purposes, linking north with south, east with west, and providing
access to the sea. This ancient bridge,[4] the elegant Mosque, the

4. The bridge was destroyed by Croatian Defence Council units during
the Bosnian War, on 9 November 1993 at 10.15 am.

various Turkish houses and the the Harem of Sultan Abdul Aziz provided startling contrast to what we had left behind in Medjugorje. If I found Mostar one of the more beautiful towns I have seen, this may have been because of the makeshift mediocrity of surroundings in Medjugorje.

The two families in our group who had been here some years previously did not recognise the place now, there had been so much hasty construction in the meantime. At the centre of everything is the church, a simple and impressive building with two towers, a wide piazza and a walk-way all around. Village life and the programme for visitors centres around this church. Loudspeakers in the towers relay whatever is happening inside the church and these can be heard in every part of the village. Behind the church a large extension like a glass-domed conservatory allows for outdoor masses with huge crowds in attendance. The scenery around about is rugged mountainous territory with brilliant blue skies and colourful sunsets. The climate is hot in summer, 106 degrees inside our hostel rooms in June. July and August are even hotter. Only one building in the village had air-conditioning. This was a café which served drink and had a TV, so it was not quite clear whether it was part of Our Lady's plans for her village.

Most of the population of the region had to emigrate to Germany to find work before the visions happened. Now they are all employed by the tourist industry. Apart from the construction programme and the hostelries, there are taxis, shops and stalls. The economy is dependent upon the visionaries. An older generation of local women wear black with head scarves. Most have a sallow skin, deeply wrinkled and wizened surrounding prayer-blasted eyes.

Pilgrimage means that this horde of visitors has been uprooted from their daily lives and transferred from sometimes grim monotony in their ordinary routine to a special place, a place where they genuinely believe that two worlds meet. Because they are all so likeminded and full of religious expectancy, they experience together a warm sense of community with complete openness to each other and to an unseen world. These are Catholics coming out of the closet and wandering around the street saying rosaries and praying in public in expansive manner without fear of being ridiculed or regarded as lunatic.

It is difficult and perhaps unnecessary to criticise, even to the point of censure, such obviously successful and enjoyable assemblies of genuine prayer. If people want to go on such holidays, why not? Leave them alone and let them enjoy themselves. They could be involved in more harmful and objectionable pastimes. Why scrutinise their enjoyment? How can it be wrong? It does no harm to anyone else. Why not leave them alone and stop trying to point out the error of their ways?

I joined every exercise listed, and performed the prescribed rituals which make up the bulk of each day's activity. From the first morning I felt depressed by the setting and the atmosphere. Everything about it seemed pink and blue, probably because of the cloudless blue sky with blazing sun on red tinted buildings, but also because of the Marian bazaar. Grotesque bad taste in every genre, not just in pictures, cards, books and statues, with all the identifiable repository kitsch to be found in every Marian shrine around the world, but also in the recently commissioned stained glass and stations of the cross in the church. The statue in the sanctuary looked like a figure of Christ on the cross but there wasn't any cross. It was a massive, barrel-chested semi-naked giant, arms outstretched like some bellowing pugilist, something as raucous and belligerent as a TV wrestler or an overfed Native American brave from one of those racist movies of the fifties.

There was a Serbo-Croatian Mass at 7.15 am and from that time onward, on the hour, every hour, a Mass in some language of one of the groups present, with no room whatever at any time in the church. You had to elbow your way inside and stand in one of the aisles. People bequeathed the precious seats in the centre to one another as if they were on centre court at Wimbledon. The English speaking population was so large that their Mass was usually outside and at midday. The forty, or so, priests concelebrating under the umbrella-like dome over the sanctuary kept the rest of the multitude ('mad dogs and Englishmen') standing in the heat for over an hour and a half, mostly to endure sermons which went on and on. My Irish farmer friend said it was 'the Americans who changed this whole style into a kind of confessional biography of their conversion to Mary, showing the local amadáns how things should be done.'

One such was an American professor of theology who gave his sermon on Mary's personal motherhood to him, how she fed him in the womb, then breast-fed him, how she looked after him especially when he was sick or feverish and he always looked forward to his 'Mom' coming into his room to see was he okay … Between him and the ranting cowboy leading the hymns like an ecclesiastical Burl Ives with all the pre-Vatican II hymns such as 'Soul of my Saviour' and 'Hail Quee-heen of Heaven', I defected to another Mass in French. Here a smaller congregation, inside the church, was addressed by an elderly priest, looking rather like Teilhard de Chardin, who stressed in a short refined homily Our Lady's right to 'Visitation' anywhere and at any time.

The inevitable consequence of the numbers at the shrine was the constant noise even inside the church. There was no moment of total silence during the day. Quite apart from the talking and bustling of the huge crowds there was a constant blare of multilingual sound from loudspeakers trying to convey to the crowds outside what was happening inside the church. Words such as *'moli'* (pronounced Mowlee), *mico* (as in microphone) and *mir* (meaning 'peace'), three Serbo-Croatian sounds which kept rasping through the loud-speakers from raucous and tuneless male voices: *'Mico, mico, mico Maria'* endlessly, endlessly. The *Mirecorder* is one of the prominent organs of Our Lady's message.

On the other hand, it is impossible not to witness the atmosphere of celebration present everywhere. Even if it was too crowded to enjoy any kind of seclusion and private prayer, there was a kind of excitement and general worship of a congregational nature which must have been prayerful for many pilgrims. This would have been especially true of the 'folk groups' which sang in the evenings in the public square. The relief from heat and the excitement of evening, as the only time when activity was possible without discomfort, allowed these sessions to continue until late. The lead singer was an ex-rock star who had forsaken the fleshpots and devoted himself to Our Lady. He did have a pleasant voice and arranged the various tediously popular tunes in ways that made them less banal and available for crowd participation. These sessions usually ended with a number of public confessions, such as a former IRA man who admitted to having killed several people, flanked by a former member of the UDR who accused himself of similar crimes. Neither could forgive the other but the consensus was huge admiration for Our Lady for having brought them so far. At these sessions some older people cast aside their normal inhibitions, dancing around and singing in ungainly and embarrassing abandon. There was an atmosphere of self-congratulatory connivance between the large number of young people and the older generation: the young thinking condescendingly how nice it was to have the wrinklies letting down their hair; while the oldies felt it was like the good old days when young people enjoyed simple pleasures instead of grannybashing and drug-pushing. This somewhat stale air of self-congratulation provided most of the impression of general well-being.

Excitement is provided at every turn by the possible occurrence of supernatural events. Apart from the daily appearance of Our Lady to whichever visionaries are present in the church, whether in the organ loft or the sacristy, which is attended by the privileged few, while the masses peep through the windows to see if they can see someone who sees someone who sees Our Lady, these days were the important anniversary when Our Lady was supposed to appear and give a message. On 25 June 1990 (on the same day that Ireland beat Romania in the World Cup by penalty goals) we all (200,000 of us) walked up the mountain of apparition (*podbrdo*) at 10.30 pm. One of the nuns in our house had been there since 6.30 pm in case she wouldn't get a good view and, in fact, I was just beside her when I arrived four hours later. There were old people, cripples, babes in arms and then just thousands crushed together on the mountainside with hardly room to move. It was impossible to go forward or backward until the whole mob began to move down the mountain again. We stayed there until well after midnight. Waves of AVE AVE AVE MAR EEEE AAA would sweep up towards us and then someone nearer to the scene would tell them to shut up. Every shooting star and movement in the sky was greeted with applause. Eventually after so many rosaries, the mountainside began to move down to the village again. It was a really terrifying experience climbing down a rocky mountain in the dark. There were torches, but people stood on other people and fell into bushes and over stones onto their knees. How we ever reached the village intact is the real miracle. If there were any accidents we never heard about them. Apparently Our Lady did appear even though nobody had seen her and she relayed the following message which was the talk of the village as soon as it had been translated into every language present on campus: 'Dear children, today I desire to thank you all for your sacrifices and for all your prayers. I am blessing you with my special motherly blessing. I invite you to decide for God so that from day to day you will discover his will in prayer. I desire, dear children, to call all of you to a full conversion so that joy will be in your hearts. I am happy that you are here today in such great numbers. Thank you for your response to my call.' These banalities were read out and preached about at every Mass until the end of my stay.

Next we visited the visionaries. Our group was told to meet beside a certain statue at a certain time so that we could sneak off to Vicka's house where she would be meeting the English-speaking group. Nobody else was to be told except us in case the whole 200,000 might arrive. We got to the appointed place: a small courtyard with a covering of green vine leaves leading onto a street. The courtyard was packed like a tube-train at rush hour and crowds milled around pouring out onto the street. I was inside the courtyard which at first I thought a privilege.

Vicka stepped out from the balcony of her two-storey house and down some steps leading to the courtyard. The crowd cheered. She had a fresh complexion and dark hair. A childlike but sensuous mouth kept smiling unpretentiously. She welcomed everyone with delicate hands waving. She spoke, and the guide began to translate into Italian. We were there at the wrong time. There was no way of getting out. We had to stay and endure the Italian fans who were quite hysterical. Several climbed onto the balcony encircling the girl to have a photograph taken; others insisted on handing her petitions themselves; all of these were determined to touch her. Around me the Irish contingent was highly critical, saying quite openly that it was a disgrace to let such people into her courtyard, who had an entirely materialistic and commercial view of the visit.

When eventually they were asked to leave and make room

for the English-speaking visitors, they simply refused to move. They were not going to be shunted out of the presence of the visionary until they had done a hell of a lot more touching and screaming and until at least two more photographs had been taken of their whole family with the girl who saw Our Lady every day. The Irish fans, known as the most ruly fans in the world, began to get the message. If you want to get the Italians out of the goalmouth you have to shove. So began the most un-wieldy scuffle during which both sides howled *Aves* as a war-cry and the crowd in the courtyard began to wheel in a circle as both sides tried to remove the other. Eventually the poor girl causing this mass movement left the stairs and retired into her house saying that she would not come back until order had been restored.

For those of us who felt that all would be solved once we had rid ourselves of the Italians, a rude shock was on the way. The girl came back on to the steps and she looked even more beauti-ful up close – I was within feet of her at this stage. She began to speak and a boy translated. She was wearing a red cotton T-shirt and jeans. She had a kind of annulled sensuality and wonderfully deep, old, compassionate, emblazoned eyes. As she talked serenely about Our Lady, the crowd fought, shoved and swore at each other trying to reach her, give her petitions, stand beside her, touch her, kiss her. It became frightening at one point and we were amazed to realise that most of these contestants were Irish. These pilgrims assumed a glazed determination and pushing for their county with fistfuls of local petitions, they set off through the masses of people to reach the slender girl who was as near to Our Lady as they were ever likely to get. So, we were just as bad as the Italians.

During the 'Any Questions' time there was a man who kept asking if his father was in heaven. He had, apparently, spent the whole week asking each visionary the same question so they were ready for him. Vicka told us that Our Lady wanted us to fast on bread and water every Wednesday and Friday, we were to make sacrifices, say the rosary and go to Mass. She described heaven, hell and purgatory. The first was golden and tri-coloured, the second was full of twitching people and the third had a fire in the centre and those who went through it were human beforehand, but after the ordeal they were distorted monsters. On this happy note we were told we had half an hour to get back to the church for Mass and that Our Lady really wanted us to be there.

The second visionary was Ivan who must have been about twenty years of age. He was more sultry and nonchalant, looking like a prelate and lacking the charm of the other visionaries. He was writing a book for young people. The scene around his house was similar except that there was more room as he lived out in the open countryside. The third visionary I visited was Jellina Vasilj (18 years of age). She did not see Our Lady but had 'inner locutions' and heard her voice. She wore a T-shirt with 'Pittsburgh Folk Festival' on the front and was given the same treatment about the Irish gentleman's father, and photographed with eight portly Italian ladies before she began her address. She looked tired, drained, passive but peaceful. She was dignified with the same kind of rapt eyes.

I was convinced that these three people were genuine and that they did have visions or locutions. They were certainly not lying as the Bishop of Mostar seemed to imply. However, I do not believe that Our Lady was actually appearing to them. What we have here is a phenomenon somewhere between subjective delusion and objective appearance. This is the projection from the unconscious of both the visionaries and their community. This need not mean that the Holy Spirit is thereby excluded. It is a work of religious imagination which cannot be dismissed as mere imaginings. Henri Bergson describes the popular piety which engenders and surrounds such manifestations as a 'mediating image'. It is given to certain intense and creative temperaments as sometimes the only means whereby they can grasp their faith in a way that is capable of influencing their lives. As Jean Guitton suggests:

> It is certainly possible, in creative invention, to dispense with this 'mediating image' just as it is possible to dispense with 'private devotion' ... Some people will think this the wiser course, more conformable to reason and more worthy of the God we worship ... Certain minds, akin to those of the monks of old, stand in positive need of the bare and un-

adorned. To them, what is arid and rarefied supplies the place of those helps which others need to seek in imagery and emotional fervour … They find themselves ill at ease unless it be in a desert or a monastery of Trappists. It is undeniable that devotions often make for superstition, and that for many they are an actual hindrance to the true religious spirit … When seen from outside, or isolated from their living source, many of these devotions are barely defensible. The clergy are suspected of tolerating what they are unable to suppress: the malicious suggest that there is a profit-motive behind it all … It should be noted too – as Plato observed – that there are certain inferior means of cognition that procure, for the majority, more enlightenment and truth than do those that are purely abstract and intellectual.[5]

I do not doubt the good faith of the visionaries, the priests who support them, the village community of Medjugorje, and the thousands of people who have journeyed to this place over the years. I believe that there were / are visions, and that 'apparitions' do occur. However, when dealing with the visionary imagination one must make important distinctions between the energy of such manifestations which testifies to the presence of an unseen world and our communion with those who dwell there, and the 'forms' in which and through which such energy creates the mediating image which, in its turn, so often reflects the narrow and impoverished limitations of the religious culture from which it emerges.

And here, the danger is that the 'forms' emanating from Medjugorje try to imprison people in a conservative, reactionary straitjacket, no longer attuned to twenty-first century 'signs of the times.' The overriding emphasis in Medjugorje is return to spiritual childhood. This, in itself, could claim to be scriptural in origin but not when it interprets this word 'child' as infantilism. Unable to create a coherent world of faith for the times in which we live, this option favours a return to a Marian devotion which is frozen in the past, and which encourages a prepubescent piety oblivious to the world and century in which we live. Instead of living in the real world of the twenty-first

5. Jean Guitton, *The Blessed Virgin*, 1949, pp 6-7.

century and carefully reading the signs of the times for dis-
cernible messages from the Holy Spirit, such 'children of Mary'
prefer to ignore the sacramentality of the world they live in and
to search for other 'messages', for signs and wonders from another world, for visitations from otherworldly, all-powerful and
reassuring beings. There is a huge difference between genuine
spiritual childhood and infantilism. Medjugorge risks being a
Disneyland for the children of Mary. And in such a context, the
words of *Lumen Gentium* [#67] from the Second Vatican Council,
on the cult of the Blessed Virgin in the church, are relevant. This
document strongly urges theologians and preachers of the
Word of God, to be careful to refrain from all false exaggeration:

> Following the study of Sacred Scripture, the Fathers, the
> Doctors and the Liturgy of the Church, and under the guid-
> ance of the Church's Magisterium, let them rightly illustrate
> the duties and privileges of the Blessed Virgin which always
> refer to Christ, the source of all truth, sanctity and devotion.
> Let them carefully refrain from whatever might by word or
> deed lead the separated brethren or any others whomsover
> into error about the true doctrine of the Church. Let the faith-
> ful remember moreover that true devotion consists neither in
> sterile or transitory affection, nor in a certain vain credulity,
> but proceeds from the true faith by which we are led to
> recognise the excellence of the Mother of God, and we are
> moved to a filial love towards our mother and to the imitation
> of her virtues.

The words to be emphasised here are 'sterile or transitory affection' and 'vain credulity' both of which apply to Medjugorje.
The other important emphasis is on ecumenism. The supporters
of Medjugorje hold that the 'messages' of peace being transmit-
ted here are all-embracing and ecumenical to the point that
some concern was being shown in Rome about a possibility of
religious indifference. The message certainly is 'peace' and, as
René Laurentin points out, 'these messages refer to a very concrete reality: the atmosphere of hostility, contempt, religious
warfare, which dominates many Croation villages.'[6] However,

---

6. René Laurentin, *Ten Years of Apparitions*, Milford OH: Faith Publishing
Co, 1991

even if it is true that the message is tolerance, ecumenism, peace, the medium is likely to lead … 'into error about the true doctrine of the church.' If, as is claimed, there have been several visitors to Medjugorje from other religions and denominations who have been convinced by the 'messages' being preached, this could also represent a prevalent fundamentalist ecumenism between all those in the world today, from whatever creed, culture or religion who believe that the contemporary world has gone to hell and that the only future for religion is a return to fundamentalist and puritanical simplicity. Such is the battle which everywhere rages between those believers who move forward to find faith in the twenty-first century and those who hold that our only hope is to return to the spiritual structures of the nineteenth century.

However, it is not enough for those who are in authority and charged with 'rightly illustrating' the duties and privileges of the Blessed Virgin, to stand back and condemn as mass hysteria or hypnotic thraldom the events which have been happening in Medjugorje for nearly thirty years now; nor is it effective to forbid people to go there or organise pilgrimages to such a site. Such prohibitions only increase the popularity of the pilgrimage for those who find no difficulty about the choice between obedience to the bishop or to the Blessed Virgin Mary. More important than banning food which people enjoy is provision of satisfying alternatives. We again must distinguish between the essential religious energy of a people and of a person, and the mediating images which are needed to illustrate the truth. In the cinema, directors like Fellini and Bunuel have been showing us for over half a century the kind of false and idolatrous images which have been allowed to prosper in our communities. Instead of paying attention to these and other creators of 'masterful images' and harnassing the newly invented medium of the image, which is the cinema, the church has stood back and, for the most part, condemned both the medium and the message. Meanwhile these image makers of the twentieth century have turned their invention into an industry: their religion has been more effectively packaged and distributed than any other in the history of the world. They have an altar and an icon in nearly every home in the Western world. The television (with the 'vision' matching up to anything that Medjugorje has on offer) has become a place of worship. And still church authorities continue to be suspicious of and condemn contemporary image makers. The cathedral, the fresco, the icon, the mosaic, works of art of other centuries were all used by the church to spread the word of God, and these should, in the twenty-first century, have found their parallels in the cinema, the poster, the photograph, the advertisement. If the energy, the religious fervour, the devotion, and the love, which have all been so obviously present in Medjugorje over the last quarter of a century, had been harnassed to the artistic and theological vision of the church, what kind of Chartres or Santa Sophia might not now adorn the mountains of Bosnia-Herzegovina?

As it is, the phenomenon is long in devotion but short in vision; nor is this the fault of those who are called there. Until the gospel (the local people in Medjugorje call the Virgin Mary 'Gospa') is presented to all people with the same fullness, immediacy, excitement and 'vision' as is experienced by those who visit this paraliturgical site, what right has anyone to ask them to leave? Unless Christianity can capture the popular imagination of ordinary people, it has failed the original creative artistry of its first ingenious preacher.

Nor am I suggesting that the church become more Medjugorjeous than Metro-Goldwyn-Meyer; I am saying that the church has, for historical reasons, neglected a whole area of its life between the theological and the devotional, which is the area of spirituality where 'mediating images' grow. We have neglected, to our cost, the fourth transcendental which is a legitimate road to God, the way of beauty, the way of art. And art is the medium which, in the twentieth century, became one of the most popular and spectacular phenomena reaching every human being in shape, form, or image. 'Mass media' is a term which could have meant something more purposeful today if Michelangelo and Andrei Roublev had been pioneers of its emergence, instead of signifying, as it does for many religious people, Mammon, or whatever costume the contrary opposite to God now wears.

I am not throwing up my hands and saying that we have lost the battle. On the contrary, the message of Medjugorje to me is that the sap is still green, religious life is still alive and well and bursting its banks; even if it is a century later than it might have been, it is still the time to build those hydro-electric power-stations which can harness and channel this superabundant energy.

Medjugorje has all the ingredients of a block-buster movie. Apart from the apparitions and revelations, apocalyptic phenomena are a dime a dozen. One of the nuns in our house could not tell us the amount that Our Lady had done for her during her stay: a full-sized Sacred Heart had danced upon one of the crucifixes on the mountain for her private delectation. The Dublin scrap-merchant and his wife saw the sun revolving. This and having your rosary beads turned into gold are some of the lesser manifestations of divine approval. There is a warning in the official Topflight Guide to Medjugorje coming directly from Dublin eye specialists: 'Irish pilgrims have been encouraged to gaze at the sun for varying periods of time. Some have suffered blurring of vision which required medical attention on returning home and some have suffered permanent damage to vision.' Such blurring or damage to vision is what one risks when exposed to the full naked energy of the sun. It was and it is the role of the church to place a mediating filter for the faithful instead of forcing them to gaze at raw reality, or telling them that they have no right to go out at all into the sun.

As a resort in a consumer society where religious holidays can be as profitable as any others ('happy holiday with heaven thrown in') what objection can there be to Medjugorje as a package-tour pilgrimage?

From the point of view of the host country, it seems dangerous to have so many people depending for their livelihood on this particular phenomenon. The whole economy of Medjugorje depends upon the apparitions. It would have taken a very honest and courageous official to announce that Our Lady had failed to turn up for her gig on the night when 200,000 of us were on the mountain. The pressures to produce sensational evidence are too intense to be healthy.

From the point of view of the punters, it's everyone to their own taste in matters of religious sensibility: some like it hot, some distinctly cool. If you're into Neon Madonnas then Medjugorje is the all-in holiday package for you. The trouble is that most of the believers were there on a proselytising agenda. Some bring friends or family members who are having a bad time or are going astray. Others bring their spouses to get them back on the straight and narrow: turn them into a child of Mary and eliminate ruthlessness, materialism, promiscuity. Such psychological blackmail is nearly always counterproductive, especially when the hostage is kept in a cell without air-conditioning at a temperature of 106 degrees. I met three such beneficiaries who said they were suffocated by at least three kinds of heat, would never go near the place again, and had been put off all religion for life. One husband was reading a paperback novel called *Sacred Sins*, between the rosaries, the Masses and the visions: 'There's no escaping the sizzling heat of the Washington summer', read the blurb, '... or the twisted ministry of 'the priest' – a madman who is strangling slender pretty blondes with the white silk stole of a priest, leaving notes that forgive his victims.' A telling mix of genres.

On our way back to the airport we were invited to say rosary after rosary in gratitude for the wonderful time we had had. The bus passed spectacular scenery on the Croatian coast of the Riviera. As we peered over the steep cliff the largest nudist colony in the world stretched out before us. The lady from New Orleans passed her opera glasses to the farmer from Tipperary who was heard to mutter: 'I can't get these bloody things to focus.'

CHAPTER NINE

## *Lough Derg: The Island Within*

If the whole of Ireland could not become a paragon of the kind of virtue outlined for us as a new nation state, there was a place contained within it which could act as vicarious substitute. 'Since the early days of Christianity, it has been the custom of saints and holy ones of God to withdraw from time to time into the desert, there to commune with him in solitude.' Naturally, the places selected are suited to this purpose and Ireland has many sacred sanctuaries of this kind. There is one such island among forty-six in a small lake called Lough Derg situated in the mountains of south Donegal.

Many of these islands are no more than rocks appearing above the surface of the water and all but two are uninhabited.

'From the earliest times these islands were used by the Irish saints as places of retreat. Tradition tells us that St Patrick often visited them to spend there some time in prayer and contemplation. During one of these retreats God deigned to allow him to witness the pains of purgatory and the glory that awaited the just on their deliverance therefrom. In gratitude for this favour, the apostle built a church beside the cave wherein he had received the vision, and left monks in charge. A monastery soon sprang up, and so began those penitential exercises that have continued even to the present ... An account of the vision seen here by an Irish knight named Owen is given by Henry of Saltrey, a Benedictine monk of Huntingdonshire. This being translated into several European languages, greatly increased the fame of St Patrick's purgatory. In the year 1153 the knight Owen, having quit military service on the continent, was filled with remorse for the irregularities of a soldier's life. He set out for Lough Derg and by a retreat of fifteen days in the island monastery he prepared himself for enclosure in the cave.

Once inside the cave he was shown in graphic detail the pains of hell, the sufferings of purgatory and eventually the beauties of Paradise. After 24 hours in the cave he was "received with joy by the Prior of the Island". Whatever be the true account of Owen's vision, the fame of the purgatory was increased by Henry's narration, and from every part of Europe the faithful flocked to Lough Derg. At the beginning of the nineteenth century an average of 10,000 pilgrims were visiting the site every year. At the beginning of the famine year 1,300 pilgrims arrived in one day, the total for the year being 30,000. The cave no longer exists and even the site where it used to be is contested. Pope Alexander VI ordered it to be destroyed in 1494. Long has the purgatory been regarded as the holiest spot in "holy Ireland", therefore, on landing, the people literally "put off the shoes from their feet". Nor are they resumed until the pilgrim is ready to leave.'[1]

Joseph Timoney's pamphlet on Lough Derg for *The Fermanagh Herald* written in 1926 takes up the same theme: 'It is a Holy Isle where sin and sorrow never dwelt; a haven of peace, where nothing evil ever entered, another world, where souls find final rest, because they rest in God, secluded from the tumults of the world – a sanctuary of peace, prayer and penance.' The ideals which had been suggested as possible for the whole of Ireland are at least possible on this island within the island which becomes the ideal template for our spiritual lives. The tradition of the three day Lough Derg pilgrimage, which continues to this day, entails fasting, walking barefoot, and keeping continuously awake for a period of 24 hours. 'This centuries-old practice still exists today,' the website tells us, 'allowing people to, in a sense, pray with their whole body – "This is my body, I give for you".'

The pilgrimage exercises are made up of a prayer sequence called a 'Station'. This is a well-known Celtic form of prayer, involving physical movement accompanied by 'mantra type' prayers. Nine Stations are completed on Lough Derg over the three-day period. Five Stations are made in the open air on the

---

1. James F. Kelly 'The Pilgrimage to Lough Derg', *The Irish Rosary*, September 1907, pp 665-672.

'Penitential Beds' while pilgrims say the prayers of a further four Stations together in the Basilica during their first night. The central penitential exercise of the pilgrimage is the Vigil; each pilgrim stays completely and continuously awake for 24 hours, starting at 10.00 pm on the first day. Pilgrims have one 'Lough Derg Meal' of dry toast or oatcakes and black tea or coffee on each of the three days of the pilgrimage.

In the great divorce between the church and artists in Ireland, this island in Lough Derg becomes something of a litmus test with which to gauge the antagonism between the two warring parties. Such is the intuition of Peggy O'Brien in her book *Writing Lough Derg*, in which she examines writings from various artists from William Carleton to Seamus Heaney.[2] Her take on the above quote from Timoney is that: 'This is the voice of political isolationism filtered through fervour. These are claims for Station Island, although he might have been speaking of Ireland, so locked in place is the synecdoche by this point [68].' She goes further to suggest that 'Lough Derg emerges as the quintessential symbol of an Ireland essentially defined as home to an undiluted Catholic race [69].'

Station Island in Lough Derg becomes the flagship for a 'theocratic culture, which suppressed all hints of heterodoxy,' and which swapped one kind of oppression for another as it 'marked the eerie fulfilment of British hegemony'. Her version of what I have been describing in previous chapters is that 'the newly independent state sought a semblance of unity through the invention and imposition of an idea of unsullied Irishness'. This is what she describes as 'ersatz racial purity' which often results in 'cultural xenophobia'.

And O'Brien finds in Lough Derg as regards literature what I am using it for here in terms of spirituality: 'I regard the cumulative text of Lough Derg as an ecosystem through which the evolution of Irish literature in the last two centuries may be studied [27].' Lough Derg becomes the thermometer to take the spiritual temperature of Ireland as a whole at any given moment of her history: 'Lough Derg works tend to emerge, like eruptions on the body, at times of intense cultural and personal pres-

---

2. Syracuse University Press, New York, 2006. For the remainder of this chapter I shall refer to this work with the page number in a square bracket.

sure, hence at crucial intersections in the lives and careers of the relevant artists, and of the body politic [155].' So, her fascinating study spins a narrative about Ireland which 'threads through the Lough Derg writings of William Carleton (1794-1869), Denis Florence MacCarthy (1817-1882), Denis Devlin (1908-1959), Patrick Kavanagh (1904-1967), and Seamus Heaney (1939-), ending with a poem by Polish poet Czeslaw Milosz, who died in 2004 [xiv].'

Such a panoramic sweep covers the last two centuries, concentrating on 'Irish writers using English and writing after 1800 [xviii].' The reason why she includes Milosz is because he so often compared Ireland with Poland and is one of the poets who most influenced Seamus Heaney in terms of Catholicism at least. 'Around the time of the composition of "Station Island", Heaney is absorbing Milosz, who on many occasions compared Ireland to Poland, seeing both as self-identified Catholic countries on the edges of Europe, and both as victims of serial conquests [xv].'

Both these writers sought to recover for poetry a subtle spirituality which refused to align itself with a particular religious denomination but which also refused to be dismissed out of hand by an anti-religious fashion in the arts. 'During the eighties and nineties the common aim of Heaney and Milosz was to imbue poetry with a questioned but also felt religious impulse quite at odds with the metaphysics of modernism and postmodernism, ranging from agnosticism to atheism [164].'

William Carleton had once thought of becoming a priest in the Catholic Church. He then left and became a Protestant. For him St Patrick's Purgatory is the epitome of everything that he detests and has rejected in Catholicism. The extremist penitential war against nature which Catholicism proposes and which this particular Island Purgatory represents, is his target. It becomes the idol which he has to destroy. 'By stretching the powers of human sufferance until the mind cracks under them, it is said sometimes to return these pitiable creatures maniacs … sunk forever in the incurable apathy of religious melancholy.'[3] For him, 'Lough Derg is a site where sanity can drop away …

---

3. William Carleton, *Traits and Stories of the Irish Peasantry*, 1844, quoted in O'Brien, op. cit. p 41.

where one's masculinity is absolutely on the line. This liminal place is one, ironically, where a certain kind of perhaps spurious liminality must be resisted. Given this and the mythological weight of association with a devouring mother and the Lough Derg monster [178]' the island looms as an archetypal dragon which Carleton has to slay within himself.

Denis MacCarthy, who was born in 1817, a generation after Carleton, had been a seminarian and remained a fervent Catholic all his life. He was appointed by Newman to the first chair of literature at the Catholic University in Dublin and, in 1855, became professor of English Literature. Six months later he gave up the chair 'because of ill health and a predilection for privacy and repose'. This seems like a euphemism for retirement in face of the double allegiance which wracked his life: 'his attraction to Romanticism ... and his commitment to Catholicism.' He wrote a biography of Shelley despite the latter's visit to Dublin in 1812 where he addressed a meeting, along with Daniel O'Connell, at Fishamble Street 'to free the Irish people also from the self-limiting shackles of Catholicism [52]'. Cultural nationalism was more threatening to McCarthy than colonialism. After his death, obituarists took pains to describe him as 'a true Irish poet,' despite his living in England and the continent for twenty years of his life. 'Fate offered him the ideal vehicle for enacting this tension' when he translated the Spanish playwright Calderón's (1600-1681) play about Lough Derg, called (in McCarthy's translation) Saint Patrick's Purgatory. O'Brien sees the main thrust of this translation as recovering 'Ireland's connection to the rest of Europe [55]'.

Devlin, as an official representative of the Irish Republic's government, the new Department of Foreign Affairs, travelled the globe armed with an official image of the new nation among nations. His experience of the world outside of Ireland and his role as ambassador for the newly formed state provided the polarities with which his poetry would agonise. 'The purgatory of modernism, exemplified by the metaphysical trials of Wallace Stevens, is Devlin's site of suffering. As a diplomat, he brought Ireland to the outside world. As a poet, he brought that world back to Ireland by applying the skeptical questions posed by Modernism to the set text of Irish Catholicism [24].'

Interestingly, because it reveals a similarity of class and mind, Denis Devlin would lecture in the same university and department as McCarthy and would similarly give up the position. Kavanagh and Devlin's poems on Lough Derg would both be published in 1942, so that year becomes a particularly well recorded one. Lough Derg offered Devlin 'a natural vehicle' for his ambivalence towards 'the very bourgeoisie and government' he was paid to represent. 'Devlin gravitated, like a moth to a flame, towards subjects that symbolically intensified, to a painful degree, all the contradictions and ironies in the nation and the self that both thwart transcendence and promise its validity [108].' Seamus Deane describes Devlin's 'fascination with the European Catholic tradition and its devotional Irish counterpart' as 'a rare instance of a metaphysical poetry in a symbolist mode.'[4] Devlin uses the symbol of Lough Derg to achieve the impossible synthesis between Catholicism meaning 'whole' and 'universal' and Catholicism meaning 'local' and 'suffocating'; for him Station Island on Lough Derg became the oxymoron where Catholicism and Modernism were crucified together in his poetry.

'Somewhere in the nineteenth century', Kavanagh wrote in 1951, 'an anti-life heresy entered religion.'[5] His poem is an attack on the deeply pessimistic view of human nature perpetrated by the Catholic Church in Ireland, which he saw as 'anti-life' and which demanded that all his sexual energy 'be eliminated until expressed within the bonds of marriage'. Catholicism in Ireland was a negation of incarnation and a blasphemy against creation. Church and state were colluding in this necrophiliac distortion of Christianity. 'A wake is what is in progress in this country', and De Valera is the undertaker 'in his long black cloak.'[6] His poem on Lough Derg is also exploring 'the unresolved tension between flesh and spirit, between life and anti-life, between joyous and sorrowful religion.'[7] John Jordan sees

4. Seamus Deane, *A Short History of Irish Literature*, South Bend, Indiana, University of Notre Dame Press, 1989. p 231.
5. *Kavanagh's Weekly*, 24 May 1951.
6. Ibid 10 May, 1952,
7. Una Agnew, *The Mystical Imagination of Patrick Kavanagh, A Buttonhole in Heaven*, Columba Press, Dublin, 1998, pp 114-118.

Kavanagh as one of the few Catholic writers who tries 'to understand ... and treat with compassion' the prevailing 'perversion of the Catholic teaching on sex and marriage.'[8] Although O'Brien finds Kavanagh's poem *Lough Derg* somewhat unsatisfactory, 'insufficiently translating bile into art [23]'.

O'Brien finds in Seamus Heaney's *Station Island* (1984) a more balanced attempt to come to terms with the great divide between literature and Catholicism in Ireland, using the island on Lough Derg as poetic fulcrum. O'Brien quotes Heaney himself to formulate this equation: 'The problem for the native poet – how to assert independence against the double tyrannies of a Catholic state and an anti-Catholic literary paradigm [67].' Heaney is not satisfied with previous attempts to straddle the divide, opting to champion or revile whichever side the poet happens to cherish or abhor. 'The vision of reality which poetry offers should be transformative, more than just a print out of the given circumstances of its time and place [163].' In this balancing act Czeslaw Milosz acts as something of a mentor. 'Like Catholic Poland over the course of the twentieth century's two great wars, the idea of the Irish nation presents a tight knot of moral, political, philosophical, religious, and aesthetic problems for the artist. 'Station Island' becomes Heaney's way of thoroughly examining his moral conduct, specifically in relation to the carnage of the recent, decades-long, still unresolved Northern Troubles [xix].'

O'Brien understands Heaney's work *Station Island*, published in 1984, 'as urgent cultural, personal, and poetic work that needed to be done when it was done,' as many troubled believers in Ireland feel that they must do the Station to make sense of a difficult time, or to figure out a way forward. 'It is written both during the thick of the Troubles and at a time when Heaney had gained a never greater physical distance from them. Purgatory is the ideal site in which to locate this backward look that leads forward. Having moved to the South, to Wicklow in 1972, then on to Dublin in 1976, Heaney culminated this transition with the acceptance in 1981 of an academic position at Harvard University, which entailed spending one semester there every year [154].'

So, Heaney, like Devlin, and unlike Kavanagh, has the opportunity to distance himself from the provincial whirlpool, to

8. John Jordan, 'Mr Kavanagh's Progress,' *Studies*, Autumn, 1960.

experience the wider cosmopolitan perspective and come to terms with 'spirituality' in Ireland. 'One of the most persistent questions asked by 'Station Island,' is whether Catholicism can ever be separated from nationalism in Ireland.' Can such a place as Station Island ever rid itself of 'the tribal taboo'? Is there a possibility that this shrine could return to a previous incarnation, 'separating religious Lough Derg from its iconic, political status'? The question posed by Heaney's interrogation is 'whether the shrine can ever be rescued from its role, its most recent reification in history, as the standard bearer of the extremely conservative Catholicism essential to De Valera's vision of Ireland?' Heaney tries to shake out the implications of Devlin's European and cosmopolitan aspirations and Kavanagh's lampooning of oppressive local Catholicism. Is there a wider, more open, less restrictive Catholicism than the Tridentine devotional-based, exercise-driven, mechanical version of the faith, which actually overtakes Ireland in the early nineteenth century and comes to eclipse the more ecstatic, experiential, and to some, superstitious character of the pilgrimage in earlier centuries. He also questions the degree to which this legalistic version of religion is implicated in a similarly obedient, knee-crooking form of nationalism. Both forms of piety are intensified and rigidified by the beseiged position of Catholics in the North during the eighties. Further still, can spirituality be embraced, the religious impulse affirmed, apart from the over-defining structure of the church? Can the experience of faith, indeed even the liberating sensation of transcendence, be freed from the self-mortifying penitential exercises of Lough Derg?

Furthermore, is there a way in which Lough Derg with its fortuitous European pedigree might facilitate a finessing of the by this stage jejune dualism set up by colonialism, which chronically pits Irish culture against English? Can Europe intervene as a third term?'

Heaney's poem reworks all previous accounts of Station Island and invokes his own personal experience of pilgrimage there, what he can glean about the history, mythology, possibility of the place, and most especially its European extension through connection with Dante, 'the chief imagination in Christendom' to use Yeats' words. Opening himself to the mitigating influence of Europe, specifically in section xi where relief is found through that encounter with the imaginative, sympathetic monk "returned from Spain to our chapped wilderness", Heaney is pushed or guided towards an encounter with God which is not mediated through Irish Catholicism, but which happens without the need of any intermediary through direct mystical contact with the Divine, the possibility of achieving transcendence without having to employ any of the locally available transport systems. In assigning for the scrupulous poet's penance, the translating of 'something by Juan de la Cruz,' the surprisingly sensible monk suggests that Heaney's only sin may be a narrow and reductive idea of God. This is the deity who has been constructed over the course of Irish history to reflect the barrenness of the Lough Derg landscape, to match the quality of faith that often goes with it [175].

In the end, O'Brien finds in this poem by Seamus Heaney the possibility of a spiritual manifesto for us all. 'The genius behind "Station Island" is that of Heaney's *persona*, Sweeney, the bird man, the pagan king, who in his argument with the church as a power structure discovers within himself a source of freedom, his ability to fly … overcoming through poetry a form of cultural incarceration. Hence a new, highly individualised, nonideological, magpie construction of the identity of Lough Derg – and, by extension, of Ireland – is made as we read … a latter-day and revised Stephen Daedelus forging a conscience of rural Catholic Ireland – even more, of rural Catholic Northern Ireland [168-9].'

O'Brien believes that 'Heaney has been working for years towards making space for contemporary metaphysical poetry in the Irish literary tradition.' The fact that others fail to detect this dimension, and accuse those who suggest it as reading more into the poems than they contain, prompts this author to pursue her intuition even to interpretation of the pauses between the words, her reading between the lines: 'Indeed, the more spiritually trenchant Heaney's introspection becomes in his career, the more the silence beyond polyphony becomes his hermeneutic key [196] … These gestational, nonverbal spaces have always been the potent heart of Heaney's poetry and perhaps his residual, not fully articulated faith [197].'

O'Brien suggests that Heaney has been making space for contemporary metaphysical poetry in the Irish literary tradition. But it is also true that poetry cannot achieve this on its own. It has to be accompanied by a certain kind of critical understanding that is guarantor of its authenticity and exegete of its accomplishment. A certain kind of critical thought can facilitate the journey to and from the protectorate of poetry, and that centre of equilibrium for which poetry clears a space. Grappling irons and gang-planks are necessary for pedestrian access to the treasure trove on board. O'Brien's book has ferried us all to and from the island in a way that makes pleas of invincible ignorance about this itinerary unconvincing in the future. Ireland is now enjoying a new era of religious poetry, she affirms. 'By "religious" I emphatically do not mean Catholic, nor do I refer to any orthodoxy [264].' Her detailed and intuitive study shows that 'the Lough Derg poetry is as close to prayer as it is possible for words to come while still retaining reason and avoiding the rote ... This tradition of writings, in a sense religious *Dindsenchas*, provides a neutral but formal zone where the individual's innate spirituality can express itself without crooking the knee to church or nation [262].' So, to sum up the important questions which poetry inspired by the Lough Derg phenomenon should prompt in us:

1) Can Catholicism be separated from Nationalism in Ireland?
2) Can Spirituality be embraced, the religious impulse affirmed, apart from the over-defining structure of the church?
3) Can the experience of faith, indeed the liberating sensation of transcendence, be freed from the self-mortifying penitential exercises of Lough Derg?
4) Is there a way in which Lough Derg with its fortuitous European pedigree might facilitate a finessing of this, by this stage, jejune dualism set up by colonialism, which chronically pits Irish culture against English? Can Europe intervene as a third term? [166-7]

If we are to move forward towards a development which respects all the elements in the amalgam which we are, which we have become, which we hope to direct towards the most optimistic future, it is essential that the church collaborate with scientists and artists who are the antennae, the diviners, the creators of our future. They are our eyes, our ears, our imaginations. Listen to Seamus Heaney in 1991: 'My language and my sensibility is yearning to admit a kind of religious or transcendental dimension. But then there's the reality ... the complacency and the utter simplification of these things into social instructions. That's what's disappointing. Artists shake our complacency and refuse the utter simplification of "these things" into social instructions.'[9] One of the tasks of poetry, Heaney reminded us in his T. S. Eliot Memorial Lectures of 1986, is to resist moral cowardice. He uses examples of poets in those communist states in Eastern Europe who, until quite recently, were living in situations where art was either harnessed to government policy or else became a public enemy of state legislature and ideology. But most of us can recognise the world he is describing:

> A world where poetry is required to take a position that is secondary to religious truth or state security or public order . ... In ideal republics, Soviet republics, in the Vatican and Bible-belt, it is common expectation that the writer will sign over his or her individual, venturesome and potentially disruptive activity into the keeping of an official doctrine, a traditional system, a party line.[10]

Nor do we have to be governed by a bloody dictator to undergo such doctrinaire browbeating. 'I am thinking', he says, 'not so much of authoritarian censorship as of an implacable consensus.' The role of the poet is to expose 'to the majority the abjectness of their collapse, as they flee for security into whatever self-deceptions the party line requires of them.' Like Cezanne at the beginning of the century, Heaney has been trying to show us how to see, how to 'credit marvels'. His poetry and his criticism should become an essential part of the probing which determines the direction we now want to take. Artists are like scouts in the evolutionary march. Their work is to explore the territory ahead and advise on the paths to be tested.

---

9. Seamus Heaney interviewed by Ian Hargreaves in the *Financial Times*, 10 June 1991.
10. Seamus Heaney, *The Government of the Tongue*, London: Faber & Faber, 1988, p 96.

CHAPTER TEN

# Three Twentieth Century Popes

There are some who would ask what right has art or poetry to speak against truths that have been handed down to us by either God himself or his appointed representatives. The answer is that the church is built on the foundation of both the apostles and the prophets. These are two principles which should complement but which are often estranged. Both are necessary and at certain times one is more important than the other. The task of leadership is not to promote one rather than the other but to harmonise both. This is a task of discernment and, in the case of the prophetic principle, 'reading the signs of the times', understanding what the Spirit is saying to the churches.

Christianity believes that God became a human being and united the fullness and truth of our humanity to the plenitude of divinity. Such an equation demands the absolute truth of both partners. Whereas the hierarchy of the church were constantly defending the orthodoxy of divinity, they were at the same time denigrating and emasculating the reality of humanity. To make humanity worthy of the destiny to which it is called, the church implied the evacuation and disablement of all that made us truly and effectively human. So the essential paradox of the Christian equation was divided into two warring camps: those defending the orthodoxy of the church and those defending the orthodoxy of humanity. Church hierarchy were on one side; art and science were on the other. The task of leadership, again, is not to arbitrate between warring parties but rather to bring the truth of both sides together in a more fruitful and comprehensive whole.

Three popes in the twentieth century have tried to bridge the gap between these two principles. Pope Benedict XVI met up to 500 artists from around the world on 21 November 2009, in the Sistine Chapel, as part of an effort to turn the page on the Vatican's sometimes hostile relationship with the contemporary art world. This was intended as the first step toward a 'new and fertile alliance between art and faith,' the Vatican Museum's Director Antonio Paolucci said, and it was meant to mark a sort of 'reconciliation after the great divorce'. The event marked both the 10th anniversary of Pope John Paul II's 'Letter to Artists' in 1999, in which he spoke of the church's 'need for art' in painting, architecture and music, and the forty-fifth anniversary of Pope Paul VI's meeting with artists in 1964.

Pope Paul VI, whose papacy ran from 1963 to 1978, had a passionate interest in contemporary art and was responsible for inaugurating the Vatican Museum's department of Modern Religious and Contemporary Art in 1973, which includes works by Rodin, Kandinsky, Picasso and Chagall. Paolucci holds that the rupture between art and faith is 'incomprehensible', given the extensive collaboration between artists and the church, not least during the Renaissance.

Pope John Paul II, who was Pope from 1978 to 2005, was himself an artist. On Easter Sunday, 1999, he wrote a letter to the artists of the world. It takes a personal note and is addressed to 'you to whom I feel closely linked by experiences reaching far back in time and which have indelibly marked my life'. Such experiences refer, presumably, not just to artists and artistic works which have moved him, but to his own artistic endeavours as poet and dramatist.

The dialogue between art and religion which he hopes to promote by this letter and which he claims to have 'gone on unbroken through two thousand years of history' is not there 'by historical accident' or out of merely 'practical need'. This dialogue is 'rooted in the very essence of both religious experience and artistic creativity'. The Pope, who was also something of a philosopher, made one of the purposes of this letter to articulate that 'essential' connection between art and religion.

He begins with a traditional presentation of the artist as 'image of God the Creator'. In such a perspective God creates the world out of nothing and the artist is 'in some way' associated with this work. Metaphysically speaking, God alone creates and bestows being and the role of the artist is to manifest this being. 'He accomplishes this task above all in shaping the wondrous "material" of his own humanity.' Now, obviously, each one of us has this specific task to do in terms of our own humanity, but the Pope makes a distinction between each one of us and the artists, because 'not all are called to be artists in the specific sense of the term'. This specific sense of the term is 'the special vocation of the artist' which realises itself in their work. 'Their work becomes a unique disclosure of their own being, of what they are, and of how they are what they are.' The artist is really a craftsman – and the Pope uses the Polish word to show a lexical link between the word 'creator' and the word 'craftsman' – who shapes already existing material into forms which reveal their inner reality and communicate these to other people. In such a perspective, which is essentially the Aristotelian and later Thomistic one, of God as all-powerful creator and the world as his product, the emphasis is on causality, power and the huge and unbridgeable chasm between the created and the uncreated world, between the creator and the creature. In such a world, the artist is no more than an obedient servant, a humble craftsman, an unworthy recipient of the gift. This is the world of Being where God is everything and we are nothing.

From section 3 of his text, however, Pope John Paul makes a considerable paradigmatic shift. He starts quoting Polish poets and he introduces the notion of beauty as another transcendental, or approach to God, which is unique, specific and distinct from the metaphysics of causality. The theme of beauty is decisive for a discourse on art. In a certain sense, beauty is the visible form of the good, just as the good is the metaphysical condition of beauty. This was well understood by the Greeks who, by fusing the two concepts, coined a term which embraces both: *kalokagathia*, or beauty-goodness. On this point Plato writes: 'The power of the Good has taken refuge in the nature of the Beautiful ...' The artist has a special relationship to beauty. In a very true sense it can be said that beauty is the vocation bestowed on him by the Creator in the gift of 'artistic talent' ...'

This is the kernel and the key. It leaves itself open to several interpretations. The letter is addressed 'to all who are passionately dedicated to the search for new "epiphanies" of beauty.' The word 'epiphany' is in inverted commas and is the key word. Beauty and art become epiphanies of God in our world. That is a very different presentation of the truth of the incarnation from the one which a metaphysics of causality and power are forced to defend. But, as the Pope has said, quoting Plato, 'The power of the good has taken refuge in the nature of the beautiful.' The power of the good is being, but the nature of the good is love. There are four transcendentals. In other words, there are four really distinct yet equally viable ways to stretch beyond ourselves and to reach God. The way being valorised in this letter, and the way which in the past was somewhat neglected by the church, is the way of beauty. To present this way, the Pope in section 5 of his letter, traces the relationship between 'art and the mystery of the Word made flesh'. He does this, not by reference to the usual theologians and dogmatic statements, but by using St Francis as our guide. He calls on the later Franciscan, St Bonaventure, to explain the founder's theory of beauty: 'In things of beauty, he contemplated the One who is supremely beautiful, and, led by the footprints he found in creatures, he followed the Beloved everywhere.' There is, the Pope tells us, 'a corresponding approach in Eastern spirituality'. In other words he is breathing with what he has called 'the other lung of the church,' which is an equivalent image to the left brain in contemporary parlance. This would be the lived experience of the presence of God, not as one, all-powerful creator, but as triune, vulnerable lover; not as all-powerful, untouchable, impervious cause, but as self-surrendering, everpresent, Spirit. This is a theology of presence rather than of power, of generation rather than causality, of interpenetration in love, rather than eternal separation into created and uncreated being. Such a perspective translates itself into a theology of beauty in nature, of music in thought, of poetry in word, of liturgy in worship.

The most basic fact of John Paul II's faith and philosophy is the primal epiphany of 'God who is Mystery' in Jesus Christ. He quotes his own encyclical *Fides et Ratio* to stress that this is 'the central point of reference for an understanding of the enigma of human existence, the created world and God himself'. He reminds us that Judaism, from which Christianity burgeoned, explicitly condemned most forms of art as idols, because they acted as representation or imagery of the invisible and inexpressible God. But since God came on earth in human form, it has become possible to paint him, to write about him, to depict scenes of his

life, to present this reality in plays, films, music etc. The incarnation, as well as showing us the way, the truth and the life, has
also 'unveiled a new dimension of beauty'. He quotes Paul
Claudel and Marc Chagall describing sacred scripture as 'a sort
of immense vocabulary' on the one hand and as 'an iconographic
atlas' on the other. There is specific acknowledgement of Byzantine
art, and in particular the icon, as the inspired embodiment of
that new dimension of beauty unveiled in the incarnation. One
of the most important and exciting sentences in this letter is that
'the icon is a sacrament'. These words are emphasised by italics
and even though they are attributed to the theology of the East,
the Pope elaborates in his own words that 'by analogy with
what occurs in the sacraments, the icon makes present the mystery of the incarnation in one or other of its aspects.' The letter
ends with that crazy but wonderful line of Dostoyevsky which
the Pope hails as a 'profound insight': 'Beauty will save the
world.' 'Beauty is a key to the mystery and a call to transcendence.
It is an invitation to savour life and to dream of the future.'

Another inspirational part of this text concerns the role of the
Holy Spirit both in God, in the world in general, and in the
realm of art in particular. The Holy Spirit, the Breath (*ruah*) has
been present from the beginning, before Jesus Christ came on
earth. The Holy Spirit blows where it will. 'What affinity, he
says, between the words "breath-breathing" and "inspiration"!
The Spirit is the mysterious Artist of the universe,' he asserts,
quoting from the passage from Genesis where 'the earth was
without form and void, and darkness was on the face of the deep;
and the Spirit of God was moving over the face of the waters.'
Later he gives a more daring and contemporary quotation from
Adam Mickiewicz, a Polish poet writing 'at a time of great hard-
ship for his Polish homeland': 'From chaos there rises the world
of the spirit.' In a time of seeming chaos, both in the church and
in the world, there is space for the Spirit to move and this movement becomes articulate and receives form through the ministry
of the artist. Because the Pope holds that not only does the Spirit
work through chosen artists who believe, but 'every genuine inspiration contains some tremor of that "breath" with which the
Creator Spirit suffused the work of creation from the very beginning.' This means that 'even in situations where culture and the

church are far apart, art remains a kind of bridge to religious experience.'

Not only are artworks kinds of sacraments, but artists have a specific priesthood. The Pope quotes the *Constitution on the Sacred Liturgy* from Vatican II which 'did not hesitate to consider artists as having "a noble ministry"' and he quotes Dante approvingly when the latter refers to his own Divine Comedy as 'the sacred poem/to which both heaven and earth have turned their hand.' Through the work of artists, we are told in *Gaudium et Spes*, 62: 'the knowledge of God can be better revealed and the preaching of the gospel can become clearer to the human mind'. And finally, he quotes by name the Dominican theologian, Marie Dominique Chenu, who was silenced in the 1950s for his teachings on these points, but rehabilitated in time to become one of the major influences at the Second Vatican Council. Chenu's was the notion of 'the signs of the times' which we are encouraged to read as manifestations or epiphanies of the Holy Spirit, not just in apostolic times but in our own. The quotation here given by the Pope is highly significant. Chenu says that historians of theology must give due attention in their studies to works of art, both literary and figurative, which in their own way are 'not only aesthetic representations, but genuine "sources" of theology.' This is very strong speaking. How could a work of art be a 'source' of theology if it were not a direct inspiration of the Holy Spirit, as the scriptures have been recognised to be?

Pope Benedict XVI consciously timed his meeting with artists as a commemorative anniversary of these two previous contacts which he refers to by name. He reiterates the church's need for artists. 'We need your collaboration in order to carry out our ministry, which consists, as you know, in preaching and rendering accessible and comprehensible to the minds and hearts of our people the things of the spirit, the invisible, the ineffable, the things of God himself. And in this activity ... you are masters. It is your task, your mission, and your art consists in grasping treasures from the heavenly realm of the spirit and clothing them in words, colours, forms – making them accessible.' He reminds his audience of his predecessor's commitment to 're-establish the friendship between the church and artists,' and his invitation to artists to make a similar, shared commit-

ment, 'analysing seriously and objectively the factors that disturbed this relationship, and assuming individual responsibility,
courageously and passionately, for a newer and deeper journey
in mutual acquaintance and dialogue in order to arrive at an authentic "renaissance" of art in the context of a new humanism.'

So the purpose of the 2009 meeting with Benedict XVI is un-
ambiguous: 'With great joy I welcome you to this solemn place,
so rich in art and in history. I cordially greet each and every one
of you and I thank you for accepting my invitation. At this gathering I wish to express and renew the church's friendship with
the world of art, a friendship that has been strengthened over
time; indeed Christianity from its earliest days has recognised
the value of the arts and has made wise use of their varied language to express her unvarying message of salvation. This friendship must be continually promoted and supported so that it may
be authentic and fruitful, adapted to different historical periods
and attentive to social and cultural variations. Indeed, this is the
reason for our meeting here today.'

The Pope acknowledges that artists do not have to be either
Catholic or Christian to be inspired by the Holy Spirit: 'Today's
event is focused on you, dear and illustrious artists, from different countries, cultures and religions, some of you perhaps re-
mote from the practice of religion, but interested nevertheless in
maintaining communication with the Catholic Church, in not reducing the horizons of existence to mere material realities, to a
reductive and trivialising vision. You represent the varied world
of the arts and so, through you, I would like to convey to all
artists my invitation to friendship, dialogue and co-operation.'

He reminds the gathering of the essential link between art
and religion, between beauty and hope in the words of Paul VI:
'This world in which we live needs beauty in order not to sink
into despair. Beauty, like truth, brings joy to the human heart,
and is that precious fruit which resists the erosion of time, which
unites generations and enables them to be one in admiration.
And all this through the work of your hands ... Remember that
you are the custodians of beauty in the world.'

Nor is this a sentimental or romantic appeal to art which
might camouflage stark human realities which confront us:
'Unfortunately, the present time is marked, not only by negative

elements in the social and economic sphere, but also by a weakening of hope, by a certain lack of confidence in human relationships, which gives rise to increasing signs of resignation, aggression and despair. The world in which we live runs the risk of being altered beyond recognition because of unwise human actions which, instead of cultivating its beauty, unscrupulously exploit its resources for the advantage of a few and not infrequently disfigure the marvels of nature. What is capable of restoring enthusiasm and confidence, what can encourage the human spirit to rediscover its path, to raise its eyes to the horizon, to dream of a life worthy of its vocation – if not beauty?'[1]

This is hard-nosed recuperation of a metaphysics of art necessary for survival in our world: 'Dear friends, as artists you know well that the experience of beauty, beauty that is authentic, not merely transient or artificial, is by no means a supplementary or secondary factor in our search for meaning and happiness; the experience of beauty does not remove us from reality, on the contrary, it leads to a direct encounter with the daily reality of our lives, liberating it from darkness, transfiguring it, making it radiant and beautiful.'

And then comes an important analysis of what this might mean in practice:

Indeed, an essential function of genuine beauty, as emphasised by Plato, is that it gives man a healthy "shock", it draws him out of himself, wrenches him away from resignation and from being content with the humdrum – it even makes him suffer, piercing him like a dart, but in so doing it "reawakens" him, opening afresh the eyes of his heart and mind, giving him wings, carrying him aloft. Dostoevsky's words that I am about to quote are bold and paradoxical, but they invite reflection. He says this: "Man can live without science, he can live without bread, but without beauty he could no longer live, because there would no longer be anything to do to the world. The whole secret is here, the whole of history is here." The painter Georges Braque echoes this sentiment: "Art is meant to disturb, science reassures." Beauty pulls us

1. Pope Benedict XVI, Address to Artists, Sistine Chapel, Saurday 21 November 2009.

up short, but in so doing it reminds us of our final destiny, it sets us back on our path, fills us with new hope, gives us the courage to live to the full the unique gift of life. The quest for beauty that I am describing here is clearly not about escaping into the irrational or into mere aestheticism.

This endorsement of art as the guardian of beauty is not without its criticism of some of the ways in which art can also renege on its mandate: 'Too often, though, the beauty that is thrust upon us is illusory and deceitful, superficial and blinding, leaving the onlooker dazed; instead of bringing him out of himself and opening him up to horizons of true freedom as it draws him aloft, it imprisons him within himself and further enslaves him, depriving him of hope and joy. It is a seductive but hypocritical beauty that rekindles desire, the will to power, to possess, and to dominate others, it is a beauty which soon turns into its opposite, taking on the guise of indecency, transgression or gratuitous provocation.'

This is followed by an attempt to describe the ultimate depth of beauty and the corresponding vocation of the artist: 'Authentic beauty, however, unlocks the yearning of the human heart, the profound desire to know, to love, to go towards the Other, to reach for the Beyond. If we acknowledge that beauty touches us intimately, that it wounds us, that it opens our eyes, then we rediscover the joy of seeing, of being able to grasp the profound meaning of our existence, the Mystery of which we are part; from this Mystery we can draw fullness, happiness, the passion to engage with it every day.' Quoting John Paul II, in his Letter to Artists, Benedict XVI acknowledges that 'Even when they explore the darkest depths of the soul or the most unsettling aspects of evil, the artist gives voice in a way to the universal desire for redemption … Beauty is a key to the mystery and a call to transcendence.'

But these quotations from the past lead the present Pope to go further in an attempt to incorporate art and beauty into the necessary search for truth:

Beauty, whether that of the natural universe or that expressed in art, precisely because it opens up and broadens the horizons of human awareness, pointing us beyond our-

selves, bringing us face to face with the abyss of Infinity, can
become a path towards the transcendent, towards the ultimate Mystery, towards God. Art, in all its forms, at the point
where it encounters the great questions of our existence, the
fundamental themes that give life its meaning, can take on a
religious quality, thereby turning into a path of profound
inner reflection and spirituality.'

In his attempt to show the idiosyncratic and specific way towards transcendence which is the way of the artist, Benedict
XVI quotes Hans Urs von Balthasar, the twentieth century theologian who's life's work was an attempt to open the way of
beauty and art towards the transcendence of God:

> In this regard, one may speak of a *via pulchritudinis*, a path of
> beauty which is at the same time an artistic and aesthetic
> journey, a journey of faith, of theological enquiry. The the-
> ologian Hans Urs von Balthasar begins his great work enti-
> tled *The Glory of the Lord – a Theological Aesthetics* with these
> telling observations: "Beauty is the word with which we
> shall begin. Beauty is the last word that the thinking intellect
> dares to speak, because it simply forms a halo, an untouch-
> able crown around the double constellation of the true and
> the good and their inseparable relation to one another." He
> then adds: "Beauty is the disinterested one, without which
> the ancient world refused to understand itself, a word which
> both imperceptibly and yet unmistakably has bid farewell to
> our new world, a world of interests, leaving it to its own
> avarice and sadness. It is no longer loved or fostered even by
> religion." And he concludes: "We can be sure that whoever
> sneers at her name as if she were the ornament of a bourgeois
> past – whether he admits it or not – can no longer pray and
> soon will no longer be able to love."

But probably the most unusual and significant quotation in
this letter is from Simone Weil: 'In all that awakens within us the
pure and authentic sentiment of beauty, there, truly, is the presence of God. There is a kind of incarnation of God in the world,
of which beauty is the sign. Beauty is the experimental proof
that incarnation is possible. For this reason all art of the first

order is, by its nature, religious.' This quotation opens the possibility for art of its being a way of doing theology. It is followed in the letter by another quotation from Hermann Hesse: 'Art means: revealing God in everything that exists.'

The Pope's final plea to artists is forceful and timely:

Dear artists, as I draw to a conclusion, I too would like to make a cordial, friendly and impassioned appeal to you, as did my predecessor. You are the custodians of beauty: thanks to your talent, you have the opportunity to speak to the heart of humanity, to touch individual and collective sensibilities, to call forth dreams and hopes, to broaden the horizons of knowledge and of human engagement. Be grateful, then, for the gifts you have received and be fully conscious of your great responsibility to communicate beauty, to communicate in and through beauty! Through your art, you yourselves are to be heralds and witnesses of hope for humanity! And do not be afraid to approach the first and last source of beauty, to enter into dialogue with believers, with those who, like yourselves, consider that they are pilgrims in this world and in history towards infinite Beauty! Faith takes nothing away from your genius or your art: on the contrary, it exalts them and nourishes them, it encourages them to cross the threshold and to contemplate with fascination and emotion the ultimate and definitive goal, the sun that does not set, the sun that illumines this present moment and makes it beautiful.

CHAPTER ELEVEN

## *Artists Alone Live in the Present*

Without art we would be nothing but foreground and live entirely in the spell of that perspective which makes what is closest at hand and most vulgar appear as if it were vast, and reality itself.

— Neitzsche, *The Gay Science*, 78

We are so ensconced in our own fantasy world that we cannot unwrap all the protective layers of celluloid which cushion us into our dreams.

The chief enemy of excellence in morality (and also in art) is personal fantasy: the tissue of self-aggrandising and consoling wishes and dreams which prevents one from seeing what is there outside one. Almost all art is a form of fantasy-consolation and few artists achieve the vision of the real. But the greatest art is 'impersonal' because it shows us the world, our world and not another one, with a clarity which startles and delights us simply because we are not used to looking at the real world at all. It is important too that great art teaches us how real things can be looked at and loved without being seized and used, without being appropriated into the greedy organism of the self.[1]

It is not just individuals who allow a fantasy life to prevent them from accessing the real world. Peoples, nations, and cultures can provide a similar illusion or camouflage whether this be an ideology or a religion. The twentieth century was a battleground of ideologies preventing us from gaining access to the real world.

Most ideologies behind political regimes of the twentieth century were opposed to modern art which they saw as decadent. Artists were trying to show us the new world we had just

---

1. Iris Murdoch, *Existentialists and Mystics* (London: Penguin, 1999), 348-352.

entered. Artists not only see but they shape the world around us, they provide the composition which structures the way in which we see, hear, taste, touch, the otherwise chaotic world in which we live. Artists form what we look at and what we see. Gertrude Stein and Picasso were walking through the streets of Paris during the First World War when a camouflaged truck went by. Picasso looked at it and said, 'Yes it is we who made it: that is cubism.'[2]

The Catholic Church took a long time to enter this new world. And it shunned the artists who were making it visible, audible, tangible, preferring instead to employ 'traditional' artists who would continue to decorate the prison-house of the world that most others had left. Two French Dominican priests, Couturier and Régamey tried to get the greatest living artists to work for the church. They sought out and commissioned Leger, Chagall, Lipchitz, Lurcat, Rouault, Matisse, Bonnard and Braque to create works of art for the little Alpine church at Assy. Canon Devémy wanted Picasso to create the image of St Dominic, his fellow countryman, in this church. However, the very features which caused Hitler to condemn Picasso's art as degenerate, and Communist officials to condemn his portrait of Stalin, made the Catholic Canon withdraw also.

Modern art will have had three enemies, another Dominican said, 'Hitler, Stalin and the Pope.' 'A Group of Catholics' signed a much circulated document called *The Tract of Angers* in 1951, in which a number of painters belonging to a school led by Picasso, 'Communist Artist and Enemy of God,' were condemned.[3] *Secular Art with Sacred Themes* by Jane Daggett Dillenberger clarified for me the major adjustment which was required to change houses in the twentieth century. In fact, most people never managed the change-over but remained firmly ensconced in outhouses from the eighteenth and nineteenth centuries – especially the churches who had so many massive medieval shells to camp in. Artists were endowed with a cosmic sensitivity to the cataclysmic earthquake which had taken place below the surface and had blown away the gingham village we were trying to substitute

2. Gertrude Stein, *Picasso*, Boston, Beacon Press, 1959, p 11.
3. Jane Dillenberger, *Secular Art with Sacred Themes*, New York, Abingdon Press, 1969

for a planet floating in a void. It was only in the last quarter of the twentieth century that the news about how old the planet was, how vast the universe is, and how the human species eventually emerged etc., percolated through to a critical mass of the world's population. Up until then there were a few artists trying to show us a few home truths and trying to open our eyes and ears but they were treated as oddities or freaks of the entertainment circus.

Art can be a protest against loss of identity or integrity in the movement of the mob; it can become the programme for the people, the vision statement of a group; it can be forced to produce the architecture of the sheep-fold, the corral for the herd; it can also be, more positively, expression of individuality, of irreducible uniqueness, of idiosyncratic personal quirkiness, which may seem unusual, bizarre, outrageous, obscene, even lunatic at the time of articulation, and may cause public uproar and official condemnation, but can later reveal itself to be, not just genuine and valid expression of human being and behaviour, in the case of one particular person, but excavation of a reality which lies in the underbelly of the life of each one of us.

Culture is universal. It is the complex structure of sociopolitical, religious, educational and psychological ideologies which we enter at birth as our heritage and from which there is no easy escape. Everyone of us comes wrapped inside it. It is also particular and local. It is different for every part of the planet and at every time a child is born. So, there can be no definitive antidote. Each manifestation of it requires the particular genius of the particular place to provide its own pioneering trail-blazers who can lead the people out of bondage if necessary.

In Ireland, art as the 'other voice', has been constant and assiduous in attempting to formulate a different, a wider, a less banal and more variegated identity than the one being prescribed for us by both church and state. And the relationship between these two voices has not been harmonious, to say the least. Far from the kind of dialogue between our society and the arts, which would have been both salutary and invigorating, there developed an atmosphere of fear and suspicion which was expressed and enshrined in the 1923 Censorship of Films Act, and

the 1929 Censorship of Publications Act.[4] The censorship legisla-
tion, in the words of Joe Lee 'served the materialistic values of
the propertied classes by fostering the illusion that Ireland was a
haven of virtue surrounded by a sea of vice.'[5] Ciarán Benson,
who was himself Chairperson of *An Chomhairle Ealaíon* / The
Arts Council of Ireland, by appointment of the government of
Ireland with responsibility for funding all the contemporary arts
in Ireland from 1993-1998, wrote about 'Ideologies and Irish
Arts Policies, 1921-1991,' the year before he was appointed: 'If
the state had a responsibility for arts and culture ... its self-understanding required that it defend itself against what it understood to be the dangers of the arts rather than incorporate them
as ways in which national self-understanding might develop.'
John Charles McQuaid was sure that the Truth was already
known and that the appointment of Seán Ó Faoláin as Director
of the Arts Council in 1956 was a hindrance to the spread of that
truth. 'We shall stumble on, in the semi-gloom of minds that
have never been disciplined from youth and that have not
matured in the tranquillity of assured knowledge,' he berated
Thomas Bodkin, whom he held responsible for not 'deflecting'
Ó Faoláin's appointment. 'The modernist idea of "Truth" as a
living evolving social process was an idea waiting for its time in
Ireland. The aesthetic was emphatically subordinate to the prevailing ethic, and that ethic was unashamedly authoritarian.'[6]

The answer to creative interrogation and criticism on the part
of artists was to silence them. Many artists protested vigorously,
perhaps none more eloquently than George Bernard Shaw:

> In the nineteenth century all the world was concerned about
> Ireland. In the twentieth, nobody outside Ireland cares
> twopence what happens to her ... If, having broken England's
> grip of her, she slops back into the Atlantic as a little grass

4. An Act to make provision for the prohibition of the sale and distribu-
tion of unwholesome literature and for that purpose to provide for the
establishment of a censorship of books and periodical publications, and
to restrict the publication of reports of certain classes of judicial pro-
ceedings and for other purposes incidental to the matters aforesaid.
5. J. J. Lee, *Ireland 1912-1985: Politics and Society*, Cambridge University
Press, 1989, p 158.
6. Ciarán Benson, *Studies*, Spring 1992, p 25.

patch in which a few million moral cowards are not allowed
to call their souls their own by a handful of morbid Catholics,
mad with heresyphobia, unnaturally combining with a
handful of Calvinists mad with sexphobia ... then the world
will let 'these Irish' go their way into insignificance without
the smallest concern.[7]

The message of the artists to us, since the beginning of the
twentieth century, has been consistent, and has been repudiated
or ignored by officialdom both in the church and in the state.
And the message is this: the picture of humanity that you are
painting, whether in its ideal form or in your perception of what
it is actually like, is too narrow, too pessimistic, too 'other-word-
ly,' too unsubtle. You refuse to accept the blood-and-guts reality
of what we are, the bodily, sexual, earthy amalgam that makes
us who we are. We want to be human, fully human. If God
doesn't want our humanity the way it is, the way he made it,
then he doesn't want us at all. He wants something else. The job
of the artist is to describe, to express that reality as it actually is.
Artists have been doing that from the beginning of our history
as an independent state and because they have been doing that,
they have been condemned, banned, excommunicated by the
official organs of the church and state.

James Joyce, for instance, was a religious man. He wasn't an
atheist. He believed that the humanity being presented, en-
dorsed, canonised by the church was a fake. He gave his life and
his work to defending the orthodoxy of humanity. In a letter to
Stanislaus, his brother, in 1906 Joyce says: 'If I put a bucket into
my own soul's well, sexual department, I draw up Griffith's and
Ibsen's and Skeffington's and Bernard Vaughan's and St
Aloysius' and Shelley's and Renan's water along with my own.
And I am going to do that in my novel (*inter alia*) and plank the
bucket down before the shades and substances above mentioned to see how they like it: and if they don't like it I can't help
them. I am nauseated by their lying drivel about pure men and

---

7. George Bernard Shaw, 'Censorship', *Irish Statesman* II (1928), reprint-
ed in *Banned in Ireland: Censorship and the Irish Writer*, ed Julia Carlson,
Athens: University of Georgia Press, 1990, pp 133-138.

pure women and spiritual love for ever: blatant lying in the face of the truth'.[8]

Rainer Maria Rilke, Joyce's contemporary in Germany, made a similar protest:

> Why, I ask you, when people want to help us, who are so often helpless, why do they leave us in the lurch just there at the root of all experience? Anyone who would stand by us there could rest satisfied that we should ask nothing further from him. For the help which he imparted to us there would grow of itself with our life, becoming, together with it, greater and stronger. And would never fail. Why are we not set in the midst of what is most mysteriously ours? How we have to creep round about it and get into it in the end; like burglars and thieves, we get into our own beautiful sex, in which we lose our way and knock ourselves and stumble and finally rush out of it again, like men caught transgressing ... Why, if guilt or sin had to be invented because of the inner tension of the spirit, why did they not attach it to some other part of the body, why did they let it fall on that part, waiting until it dissolved in our pure source and poisoned and muddied it? Why have they made our sex homeless, instead of making it the place for the festival of our competency? Why do we not belong to God from this point? My sex is not directed only towards posterity, it is the secret of my own life – and it is only because it may not occupy the central place there, that so many people have thrust it to the edge, and thereby lost their balance.[9]

Throughout the twentieth century in Ireland we have been told the same thing in different ways, by innumerable artists. None of these are saying that there is no God, there is no church, there is no Christianity. On the contrary, they are suggesting that if any of these realities want to have some effective contact with us and operate any kind of comprehensive salvation, they must begin taking seriously the partner with whom they are trying to have such a relationship.

8. *Selected Joyce Letters*, ed Richard Ellmann, New York, 1975, p 129.
9. Rainer Maria Rilke, 'The Young Workman's Letter' (February 1922) translated in *Rodin and Other Prose Pieces* (London, 1986) pp 151-152.

Nor is it enough to say 'artists' and 'scientists' without reservation or discrimination. There is an ethic for the artist also, without obedience to which they become sterile, mediocre, greedy or irresponsible. There are good and bad artists just as there are good and bad bishops, good and bad scientists. And at this level, at this moment of difficulty and discovery, the role of our politicians and of the hierarchy in the church might well be to discern rather than to dictate, to peruse rather than prescribe, to exercise their authority and responsibility in a more passive way, by examining the evidence produced and expressed by the scouts and the spies, before endorsing the strategy and confirming the direction that will lead us into the second decade of the twenty-first century.

But let us trace the antagonism between art and the Establishment, in terms of church and state in the twentieth century. The Abbey Theatre, founded in 1904 by Yeats and Lady Gregory, to make sure that Irish artists need never again go to London to stage their genius, became a battleground for such antagonism. Three years after it opened, in the year 1907, it became the scene of what was later called 'the Playboy riots'. John Millington Synge's *The Playboy of the Western World* presented the Irish theatre-going public with an alternative view of Irish life. On the Monday night following no word of the play was heard from beginning to end, because about forty young men sat in the front seats of the pit, stamping and shouting and blowing trumpets all through the performance. Nor were they members of the clergy as these were forbidden to go to the theatre at all. No, we are dealing here with the essentially middle-class urban population of Dublin. They were protesting against this portrayal of Irish people and wished to 'silence the slander upon Ireland's womanhood'. Irish women would never sleep under the same roof with a young man without a chaperon, nor would they ever use the word 'shift'. Two interesting quotes from Synge point up the social undercarriage of the event: 'A young doctor has just told me that he can hardly keep himself from jumping on to a seat and pointing out in that howling mob those whom he is treating for venereal disease.' And: 'In writing *The Playboy of the Western World*, as in my other plays, I have used one or two words only that I have not heard among the country people of Ireland.'

However, for the howling mob in the audience such a representation of who they are is unacceptable.

In 1918, Brinsley MacNamara published *The Valley of the
Squinting Windows*, which so enraged the people of Delvin in Co
Westmeath that the book was publicly burnt and the author's fa-
ther, a local schoolmaster, boycotted and exiled.

In 1927, *The Plough and the Stars* of Sean O'Casey was the oc-
casion of another Abbey riot. This time it was about the slur on
Irish patriotism. By the second night of the play's one-week run,
half a dozen women in the pit stamped and hissed at intervals
during the performance. By Thursday the republicans were out
in force. Sixty-five-year-old Maude Gonne was picketing outside the door with a group of Irish Republicans. One of the
women demonstrators told O'Casey as he left the theatre that
there wasn't a prostitute in Ireland. Yeats stood up on the stage
shouting: 'Long live Ireland and Freedom of expression ... You
have made fools of yourselves again ... This play is an apotheo-
sis.' O'Casey had to look up the word and recorded in his auto-
biography: 'Did these bawling fools think that their shouting
would make him docile? He would leave them to their green
hills of Holy Ireland.' The *Irish Independent* declared that 'there
are some things that cannot be defended by invoking the name
of Art ... It is known to every constant patron of the Abbey that
in some plays words have been said and things have been
shown that would make even a tolerant censor hesitate. Ireland
may have sinned, but she has not become pagan.'

In 1942 Eric Cross published *The Tailor and Ansty*, which contained nothing in it except 'the fun and talk and the laughter
which has gone on for years around this fireside'. Not only was
the book banned for being 'in its general tendency indecent' but
copies of it were burned publicly. The tailor himself was forced
to kneel in his home while the book was burned in front of him
by two priests. There was uproar in the senate and in the Dáil,
where, Frank O'Connor recorded acidly in his introduction to
the book, 'We were all too innocent to anticipate the effect the
book would have on Mr de Valera's well-educated government.' 'When I wrote the introduction to the original edition of
*The Tailor and Ansty*', O'Connor continues, 'the models were still
alive. They were a remarkable old couple who lived in a tiny

cottage on the mountain road up to the lake at Gougane Barra ... Ansty was a beautiful woman who looked like the Muse of Tragedy but talked like a quite different muse ... The tailor spoke beautiful Irish and was like a rural Dr Johnson.'

The principal spokesman for the government banning the book was a Professor William Magennis of the National University, who saw this publication as a plot to undermine Christianity in this country. Such a campaign had originated in England, according to him, was financed by American money and was headed up by George Bernard Shaw among others.

One year later, by 1943, 2,000 books had been banned by authors including Saul Bellow, William Faulkner, Graham Greene, Robert Graves, Ernest Hemingway, Christopher Isherwood, Alberto Moravia, Vladimir Nabokov, Marcel Proust, Jean-Paul Sartre, Dylan Thomas, H. G. Wells, Emile Zola, to give an international alphabetical sample. Irish authors who were banned, from Liam O'Flaherty in the 1930s to Lee Dunne in the 1970s, included Frank O'Connor himself, the two Nobel prize winners, Beckett and Shaw, Austin Clarke, Edna O'Brien, Kate O'Brien, and, of course, Joyce.

In 1945, the organisation called *Maria Duce* was the vociferous mouthpiece for right-wing Catholic supervision of public morality. However, it was the League of Decency who, in 1957, tried to have *The Rose Tatoo* closed down at The Pike Theatre in Dublin and eventually had its director, Alan Simpson, imprisoned. He was charged with 'producing for gain an indecent and profane performance'.

Two and a half years later, *The Ginger Man* by J. P. Donleavy had to be closed after three performances at the Gaiety Theatre because of indecent and obscene references which the author refused to cut.

In 1961, Tom Murphy's play *A Whistle in the Dark* was rejected by Ernest Blythe at the Abbey because he said such people as the Carney brothers didn't exist in Ireland.

In June 1965, John McGahern's novel, *The Dark*, was banned under the Censorship of Publications Act, and in October of the same year he was dismissed from his job as a primary teacher at St John the Baptist's National School in Clontarf, Dublin.

The 1971 film *Ryan's Daughter*, written by Robert Bolt and

David Lean and based on Flaubert's *Madame Bovary*, was accused in The National Film Institute's report of showing 'Irish country girls in a disgustingly immoral light ... A film with little theme, with little regard for the true situation of the 1916 period.'

In 1977, Tom Murphy's *The White House* was screened by RTÉ television. It met a response described by Fintan O'Toole as 'the modern equivalent of the riots which greeted *The Playboy of the Western World* and *The Plough and the Stars*'. It elicited a resolution from the Youghal Urban Council protesting against 'the scandalous filth of RTÉ programmes'. Tipperary North Riding Council called it 'scurrilous and filthy'. The West Donegal executive of Fine Gael condemned it as a 'blasphemy' and 'a gross insult to Christian principles'. Cork County Council regarded the play as 'obscene' and 'absolutely disgraceful' and it was attacked in an editorial in *The Cork Examiner*.

What are all these explosive, antagonistic and negative reactions for the most part? They come from a fearful protective mechanism which hides the ambiguity, the treachery, the 'evil' inside ourselves. This works by constructing a corresponding hate object outside ourselves on which we can exorcise our panic and insecurity. We have an idealised version of ourselves and anything other than this is repressed. However, it continues to prowl the depths. Projection is the term used for throwing all the contents of that shadow onto someone else. We see and condemn in the monster outside all those weaknesses and tendencies which we fail to acknowledge or accept inside ourselves. In the Irish Catholic psyche such hate objects or scapegoats, upon which it was acceptable, even encouraged, to expend any amount of hatred were, for instance, Oliver Cromwell, Judas Iscariot, and Satan. These were the enlarged caricatures, the projected parasites, of the repressed side of ourselves, what Brian Friel called *The Enemy Within* in his play about St Columba, the archetypal paragon of Irish virtue. We have an idealised version of ourselves as we should be and Columba is one of the role models for such perfection. The rest is repressed. Such repression is more than suppression. It is more than denying or controlling urges or impulses which we actually feel in ourselves.

Repression is refusing even to acknowledge the existence of such realities. The mere entertainment of them would be too shameful to tolerate with self respect. Repression pushes even the memory of such thoughts and feelings into oblivion. An unmarried person, for instance, who believes that any thought of sexual intercourse outside of marriage is immoral may repress these sexual urges consciously until they are seemingly obliterated. However, at the unconscious level they continue to live a life of their own, which may manifest itself in hysterical condemnation of sexual indulgence in others. This sanitising process, whereby I wipe out everything that is deemed unworthy of a human being, leads to condemnation of others who fail to achieve this goal.

For Catholic-Gaelic Ireland the most obvious hate-figures are Oliver Cromwell and Judas Iscariot. They are embedded in every Irish psyche as the ultimate oppressor and traitor. Each one received the full extent of Brendan Kennelly's experience, versatility, craftsmanship and power in 1983 and 1991 respectively. His obsession with otherness, with introducing himself and ourselves to the 'enemy' we have to learn how to love, finds its most demanding and appropriate protagonists in the archetypal enemy and the icon of apostasy in the Roman Catholic Irish psyche:

> I don't think any Irishman is complete as an Irishman until he becomes an Englishman, imaginatively speaking. I was reared to hate and fear Cromwell, the legends, the folklore of my own parish, the unquestioning hatred of him, which was then transferred to England. That appalled me when I began to try to think ... Cromwell is an ordinary experiment in my own psyche: that I am giving voice to a man who made trees wither. The worst thing you can say in the part of the country I grew up in is 'the curse of Cromwell on you' and I wanted to turn that curse into a blessing.[10]

As always, Brendan Kennelly describes the success of his venture in a story:

> I got a punch in the jaw one night crossing O'Connell Bridge from a man who said 'Aren't you the bastard that had a good word for him! Aren't you the fellow that's making a hero out

---

10. Interview of Brendan Kennelly by Richard Pine, *Irish Literary Supplement*, Spring 1990, p 22.

of him?' ... And I said, 'No, he's a man, you're a man, I'm a man'. And he said: 'Drogheda!' He had all the clichés ... All of us are victims of clichés we don't even begin to suspect.

With Cromwell behind him and after eight years of 'clearing a space' within himself, he lets us hear the voice of Judas. This sounds forth in a 378 page epic. We have to marvel at the almost unlimited capacity of this poet to act as ventriloquist and I use the word in its original Latin sense of 'speaking from the belly', to evacuate such inner spaces:

> And clear a space for himself
> Like Dublin city on a Sunday morning
> About six o'clock
> Dublin and myself are rid of our traffic then
> And I am walking.[11]

This further task of unearthing the aboriginal traitor was evisceration of the most penetrating kind. We must be grateful and aghast at the capacity of this poet to haul these monsters out of our depths:

> To have been used so much, and without mercy
> And still be capable of rediscovering
> In itself the old nakedness.

In 2009, Susan Gubar wrote what she calls, a 'first' biography of Judas Iscariot from youth to old age, throughout 'the extensive span of his multimedia existence'.[12] It is a cultural biography of one of the most famous hate objects in History: the man who betrayed Jesus Christ. She explores the work of historians, artists, novelists and scholars to give an overview of how Judas has been portrayed over the centuries by different people in various cultures. The portrait is not drawn by delineating the figure or the face of her subject but by shading in the surrounding canvas until a figure emerges. However, the strange and disturbing face that appears is not Judas Iscariot's but yours and mine. Gubar's life of Judas is a reflection of his image as this has been portrayed in Western Culture since he was introduced to

---

11. Brendan Kennelly, *A Time For Voices: Selected Poems 1960-1990*, Bloodaxe 1990, p 124.
12. Susan Gubar, *Judas: A Biography*, W. W. Norton, New York, 2009.

humanity as the betrayer of Jesus in the first century of our era. The biography, therefore, is ours as much as his, from the first century to the twenty-first. She puts on display the various representations, visual, literary, theatrical, cinematic, even musical, of Judas Iscariot and comments incisively on each.

The book is not so much a biography of Judas Iscariot as a litany of the worst we think about ourselves, and which we then gather up like spitting mambas and hurl at the hate object we have placed in the stocks of our collective imaginations. Projection is a most profound and subtle psychological process which apparently colours much of what we do and say. It is difficult to detect because of its hidden nature. It is, we are told, the fundamental mechanism by which we keep our selves misinformed about ourselves. These hidden instinctual defence mechanisms are our rotating arcuballistas and levered catapults, always aimed and loaded, which we use constantly to batter to death our own worst fears about ourselves. Whatever we find threatening or unacceptable about our deepest feelings we repress and then attribute to someone else. Most of us have our own personal Aunt Sally whom we pillory for all we are worth and blame for our shortcomings and misfortunes, but when we are presented, as we are here, with a universally approved object of our wrath, and watch in detail the catalogue of missiles we have hurled at him over the centuries, we begin to get a much clearer image of how ghastly we are ourselves, and how devastating are the catapulting mechanisms of insult and injury which make up some of our sadistic and destructive psychological reflexes.

Susan Gubar has amassed a huge, brutish and often repulsive catalogue of how Christian imagination has vented its spleen on the disciple who betrayed Jesus. Even more disturbingly, she demonstrates how Judas became identified with 'Jewry' and took on the frightful torture inflicted on a people accused of being God-betrayers and killers. His name in Hebrew, *Yehuda*, is what the Israelite kingdom is also called, from which the very word 'Judaism' derives. The ugly face of anti-Semitism appears in most depictions of Judas Iscariot throughout history. He has become the scapegoat for our deepest most atavistic and racist tendencies. If Judas never existed, our psyches would have had to invent him to carry the burden of our self-hatred. Gubar shows how slender the evidence is and how tiny the basis for such a mountain of prejudice. New Testament accounts, although minimal in themselves, were sufficient to give *carte blanche* to succeeding ages to vent their bile. Reading what Martin Luther and even Karl Barth wrote about Judas is stomach-turning stuff. But Gubar's biography purports to show a certain maturity in our twenty centuries of vituperation, wherein we progress from regarding Judas as a loathsome pariah, to even regarding him as something of a misunderstood idealist, a rebel without a cause. Revisionists tend to ascribe to him sociopolitical awareness instead of an overdose of avarice and greed.

Using a somewhat implausible, yet nonetheless thought-provoking, juxtaposition between The Little Book of Judas and Althusser's 1969 presentation of ISAs (ideological state apparatuses) she reads Kennelly as a prophetic voice describing Christy Hannity, as it emerged in Ireland during the twentieth century, as an institutional embodiment of the spirit of Judas rather than the spirit of Jesus. Everywhere in our churches, our schools, our banks, our politics, our legal, family, trade-union, communications and cultural systems, the Judas-effect of greed, avarice and betrayal are more in evidence, as recognisable hallmarks, than are the ethos of the Sermon on the Mount. It is a sobering thought; and this book makes for sobering reading.

A dialogue must happen between artists and the church. Much has to change, many anachronisms need to be discarded, many superstitions purified, many fears allayed. We are a different, more affluent, better educated population than ever before. We need a relationship with God and an understanding of Christianity which would correspond to and connect with the reality of who we are. Artists have always claimed to be in touch with the people, their art found its source in this reality, which was often the reason why it was condemned in the past. The dialogue between who we are and who Christ is will lead us all to a fuller and more comprehensive way of being. Christianity has presented Christ as an image, as a model, as a picture of perfection. This is precisely the problem. Christianity turned itself into a pursuit of perfection rather than an achievement of completeness.

CHAPTER TWELVE

## Underground Cathedrals

Because God's children are human beings – made of flesh and blood – the Son also became flesh and blood. For only as a human being could he die, and only by dying could he break the power of the devil, who had the power of death. Only in this way could he set free all who have lived their lives as slaves to the fear of dying.

We also know that the Son did not come to help angels; he came to help the descendants of Abraham. Therefore, it was necessary for him to be made in every respect like us, his brothers and sisters, so that he could be our merciful and faithful High Priest before God. Then he could offer a sacrifice that would take away the sins of the people. Since he himself has gone through suffering and testing, he is able to help us when we are being tested.[1]

My proposal is that, at this time, the Holy Spirit is unearthing an underground cathedral in Ireland which could help to replace the pretentious, over-elaborate Irish Catholic architecture of the twentieth century. An underground cathedral is a metaphor which describes an alternative place and time of worship. It provides a setting and a framework for space and time as these can be articulated more accurately and comprehensively than heretofore. Such circumferences must include both dimensions of the finite and the infinite, the temporal and the eternal, if they are to do justice to the full spectrum of possibility. It is said that Bach was the one who best understood what Luther was trying to achieve at the Reformation. He tried to replace the over elaborate and monumental clutter which had accumulated over centuries in our churches, with the removable arabesques of real people singing and making music to the Lord. This underground cathedral in Ireland has been pointed out to me over

1. Letter to the Hebrews 2:14-18 (New Living Translation).

the last number of years and it is representative of a much more intricate and extended one which is vaster than any one person could detect. But it is emblematic of something more important and indicative of a hidden artistry which might otherwise be overlooked.

At this time, the secret work of the Holy Spirit is not being done, in most countries of Western Europe, by politicians nor by church institutions. The people who are carrying the torch are mostly artists because, as Rainer Maria Rilke foretold, in destitute times we have to rely on art to show us the way forward. Now, it does not matter very much that such work goes unrecognised, that people fail to acknowledge their sources, that the Holy Spirit remains incognito. That has been the profile of the Holy Spirit since the beginning of time.

And yet, from the beginning of time the Holy Spirit, who is the feminine form of Divinity, has been present and working in creation. 'Now the earth was formless and empty, darkness was over the surface of the deep, and the Spirit of God was hovering over the waters.' (Gen 1:2) The Holy Spirit became known as Sophia, the Greek word for wisdom. Sophia, a feminine aspect of God, gives her name to certain books of the Hebrew Bible, and was a major figure in Hellenistic philosophy and religion. She was taken up by early Gnosticism and has been incorporated into the theology of both Eastern Orthodox and Western Christianity. A key passage which describes Wisdom/Sophia in the Hebrew Bible is Proverbs 8:22-31:

> The Lord created me at the beginning of his work, the first of his acts of old. Ages ago I was set up, at the first, before the beginning of the earth. When there were no depths I was brought forth, when there were no springs abounding with water. Before the mountains had been shaped, before the hills, I was brought forth; before he had made the earth with its fields, or the first of the dust of the world. When he established the heavens, I was there, when he drew a circle on the face of the deep, when he made firm the skies above, when he established the fountains of the deep, when he assigned to the sea its limit, so that the waters might not transgress his command, when he marked out the foundations of the earth,

then I was beside him, like a skilled artist; and I was daily his delight, rejoicing before him always, rejoicing in his inhabited world and delighting in the sons and daughters of creation.

From the beginning of time in every culture of the universe recognition has been made of the artistic presence and genius of this ubiquitous Spirit of God. *Digitus Dei,* digital equivalent of the work of artists. 'Between my finger and my thumb,' between the wrist and the key-board, between my hand and the canvas, there is room for another magic, no longer of my making. This was the subject of my book *The Haunted Inkwell.* I got the title from a letter in which James Joyce tells his brother Stanislaus: 'I like the notion of the Holy Ghost being in the ink-bottle.'[2] Which is another way of saying that access to this world of ours, for the Holy Spirit who democratically guides this world, can happen for artists in the space between the paintbrush and the canvas, the nib of the pen and the paper, between the tips of the fingers and the computer screen.

The Holy Spirit who cannot enter our world without the explicit permission of those who are now in charge of this planet, I refer to ourselves, the recently arrived human species described somewhat one-dimensionally as *Homo Sapiens.* After at most 200,000 years on the planet, we upstarts placed an embargo about three hundred years ago on all imports carrying the stamp of the Holy Spirit, and in our generation artists are strip-searched for signs of any such contamination. But the elusive Spirit can sometimes bypass the cyclops with even more artistic cunning. Entry for any such illegal aliens can be achieved through camouflage, impersonation or ingenious disguise. Hiding in the inkwell, this Spirit can see to it that inspiration exceeds even the

---

2. Letter to Stanislaus Joyce, 31 August 1906. *Selected Joyce Letters,* ed Richard Ellmann, Viking Press, New York, 1976, p 100. In another letter Joyce ascribes the phrase to Stanislaus himself: 'Were I to rewrite the book as G. R. suggests 'in another sense' (where the hell does he get the meaningless phrases he uses) I am sure I should find again what you call the Holy Ghost sitting in the ink-bottle and the perverse devil of my literary conscience sitting on the hump of my pen.' This is written in the context of his having perhaps been 'unnecessarily harsh' to Ireland and to Dublin and his surprise 'that there should be anything exceptional in my writing'. Letter to Stanislaus Joyce, September 1906, Ibid, p 110.

most extravagant efforts of the particular artist. The deeper that artist digs into the artesian well of the unconscious, the more easily can the ink be adulterated. Within the depth charge created by certain words or images, this poetry, this art, can facilitate the as yet unheard of to infiltrate. We can call this other dimension the thirteenth cone, the fifth province, or 'the fourth stage', the image or the name are always inadequate to the task.

It is artistic ecstasy (a word which describes how an artist can become, as we say, 'spaced out,' *ex* and *stasis* literally mean 'out of your standing' as the Irish phrase *as mo sheasamh),* which allows them to become 'outstanding' in their particular field of art.

How often do we wake in the morning and fumble for our dictaphone to record the intuition, to take down the insight, afraid that we may lose the magic, forget the idea, destroy the impulse. How long have we waited in barren desolate blankness, wondering if the Spirit had left us, despairing that our inspiration had gone forever, wandering through empty corridors of creativity to see if any scraps had been left behind. And then, all of a sudden, the inspiration comes, like a dream in the night, a bolt from the blue, a flash of white lightning, all these images which we use in our day-to-day conversation describe the arrival and departure of the Holy Spirit in our lives. 'The wind blows where it will. You do not know where it comes from or where it is going, but you hear the sound of it. That is the way it is with anyone born of the Spirit.' (John 3:8)

Artists themselves are sometimes the most reluctant to admit or to accept that their inspiration comes from the Holy Spirit. They are happy enough to acknowledge that it comes from elsewhere, not from themselves, but they rarely identify this source in a theologically specific designation. 'I didn't do it myself,' they say, 'it came to me, or it came through me.' The airwaves, brainwaves, cacodemons, daimons, elves, fairies, gremlins, hallucinogens, Ichor, Jinns, Kismet, lady luck, the muses, Nostradamus, oracles, poltergeists, Queen Mab, R.E.M., succubus and the sandman, telepathy, undines, vampires, whippoorwills, the X-factor, Yoga, or the Zeitgeist, represent a random alphabet of ways to acknowledge an unknown source, but which avoids any explicit mention of the idea of inspiration from the Holy Spirit. Such an eventuality, accepted by over 50% of the world's population as possible in the case of the scriptures for writers, or of the holy icons for painters, is a non-runner – no way – in the case of present day writers and/or artists. Such a notion is too pious, too pompous, too pathetic to be entertained even as a possibility. The only way to develop the hypothesis is to show signs of such presence in the work, or to get the artists in question to acknowledge this source.

The outline of such a structure can be sketched by taking an aerial view of the various singular lighthouses randomly dotted around our coastlines. Recently, a constellation of recognisable contour, a virtual community has emerged, which more and more regularly connects and weaves a cordon delineating the threshold of its own sanctuary.

Such a symbolic structure lies underneath the world as we inhabit it. Ireland must excavate and provide access to such an underground cathedral and thereby become both a paradigm and an example to other peoples and countries around the word who must do likewise, if humanity is to find the underground that links us all, the cathedral to which we can eventually come to celebrate our common identity. Such is the work of artists, seers, diviners, spiritual psychologists, psychoanalytical palaeontologists, who can accomplish the patient and sensitive site clearance required.

Dublin, the capital city of Ireland, or *Duibh linn*, as the name is written in the ancient annals, means a black pool. The name has psychological resonances. In 2003, the so-called Millennium Spire was eventually completed and now stands 120 metres tall in the centre of O'Connell Street. The architect, Ian Ritchie, says that this creation should be viewed as the spire of an underground cathedral encompassing the whole city of Dublin and, perhaps, the whole country of Ireland.

James Joyce, foremost pioneer of the undergound cathedral made the city of Dublin the basic geography of his works. Walkable Dublin of Joyce's *Ulysses* has almost expanded and diluted itself to extinction. Southwards it has spread to the foothills, northwards it again falls into the sea, westwards it transgresses the boundaries of itself as a county and embraces much of Meath and County Kildare. Dublin of Joyce's day would be equivalent to 'inner city' Dublin today. This 'inner' city which Joyce made famous has, however, recently developed a number of symbolic outer features which suggest that its inhabitants are at last becoming aware of the directions in which he was pointing and the areas his works undertook to investigate. The Dublin of Joyce's imagination was essentially a place of trams. Nelson's Pillar to Kingstown (Dún Laoghaire); Phoenix Park to Donnybrook; Glasnevin cemetery to Dolphin's Barn; Drumcondra to Kingsbridge Station. Half-way through the twentieth century the whole system was scrapped. Dublin was tramless for fifty years. The Bloomsday centenary of 2004 coincided with the reintroduction of two new tramlines: Sandyford to St Stephen's Green, Tallaght to Connolly Station.

*Dubliners*, Joyce's book of short stories, describes the paralysis of his native city owing to monolithic infrastructures of politics and religion which caused entrapment in alcoholism, sexual repression, poverty. Joyce left Dublin in 1904 frustrated by such oppression. He called *Dubliners* a 'chapter in the moral history of my country', an attempt to galvanise the creative energy which would help his fellow citizens to 'revolt against the dull inelegance' of the city. Dubliners were refusing to examine the 'black pool,' the darkness underpinning the veneer of their shabby respectability, the sewage system underpinning the surface topography.

A new bridge across the River Liffey was officially opened on Bloomsday 2003. This 'James Joyce Bridge' links Ellis Quay on the north of the river to Ushers Island, where the actual house of 'The Dead' in *Dubliners* is situated. The bridge was designed by Santiago Calatrava Vallas. He recently completed his design for the new World Trade Centre Transportation Hub in Lower Manhattan and later in 2010 will unveil the Agora, a multifunctional complex within Calatrava's famed City of Arts and Science in Valencia, which will be the culmination of a twenty-year design and building project that created a city from a vast wasteland. Amongst his collection of internationally recognised work is the expansion of the Milwaukee Art Museum in Wisconsin (2001), the Athens Olympic Sports Complex (2004), the Light Rail Train Bridge in Jerusalem (2007), the Quarto Ponte sul Canal Grande in Venice (2008) and the Liège-Guillemins TGV Railway Station in Belgium (2009).

The steelwork of our James Joyce Bridge was manufactured by Harland and Wolff, makers of the *Titanic*, in Belfast, Northern Ireland. It was one of the last works of this most famous shipyard which has since closed down. Finished in gleaming white, it provides not only a most elegant sculptured connection between the teeming city and the house of 'The Dead,' but also twin pedestrianised walkways which allow Bloomsday pilgrims to walk across the waters of 'anna livia plurabelle'.

The reason why Joyce had to use the style he eventually forged for himself in *Finnegans Wake* is because 'one great part of every human existence is passed in a state which cannot be rendered sensible by the use of wideawake language, cut-and-dry grammar and go-ahead plot.' He dismissed psychoanalysis because its symbolism was mechanical,[3] but this was surely because, as Ellmann suggests, 'Joyce was so close to the new psychoanalysis that he always disavowed any interest in it.'[4] He was in fact working along the same lines himself at an artistic level and was disdainful of the plodding scientists who were tapping the same sources in a much less direct and exciting way. Art was the only appropriate medium for Joyce. Medicine and science were half measures which were even less satisfactory than the religion which he had rejected.

What is it that all these people were discovering? The answer is an inner continent, the discovery of which had greater significance and repercussion than the discovery of the 'New World' by Europeans in the fifteenth century. The difference between Joyce and the psychoanalysts, for instance, was that he was discovering as an artist and therefore sought to express this reality in all its originality, subtlety and polyvalence, whereas they, as scientists, sought to conquer it by reducing it to the machinery available to their limited fields of competence.

'In Ulysses, I have recorded, simultaneously, what a man says, sees, thinks, and what such saying, seeing and thinking does, to what you Freudians call the subconscious – but as for psychoanalysis, it's neither more nor less than blackmail.'[5] Joyce was also interested in dreams, despite his distaste for Freud. He

3. Ellmann, op. cit., p 393.
4. Ibid. p 450.
5. Ibid. p 358.

described *Finnegans Wake* as written 'to suit the esthetic of the dream, where the forms prolong and multiply themselves, where the visions pass from the trivial to the apocalyptic, where the brain uses the roots of vocables to make others from them which will be capable of naming its phantasms, its allergies, its illusions'.[6] His search was in a similar direction and dimension to that of the doctors and scientists, investigating the inner world of sexuality, of dreams, of the unconscious. What he disliked was their methodology. 'I don't believe in any science, but my imagination grows when I read Vico as it doesn't when I read Freud and Jung.'[7]

On 10 December 2009, the corresponding Samuel Beckett bridge, also designed by Calatrava, was officially opened. This 120-metre long, 48-metre high construction spans the river Liffey from Sir John Rogerson's Quay near Macken Street on the south side to Guild Street at the site of the new National Convention Centre on the north side. It crosses the Liffey and opens the Docklands and IFSC to pedestrians. As the first sculpture to greet the incoming Irish Sea, it looks like the flying buttress of the Underground Cathedral. Designed as a harp lying on its side, the cable-stayed bridge certainly conveys the image of the *cláirseach*, as seen on the Irish coat of arms, coins, passports, and on a pint of Guinness. Based on the ancient lyre, the Irish harp is one of the world's oldest instruments. The characteristic features of the historical *cláirseach* or Irish harp are its strings of metal wire, usually brass but possibly also gold and silver. These are attached to a massive soundbox typically carved from a single log of willow, a reinforced curved pillar and a substantial neck, flanked with thick brass cheek bands. Usually played with the fingernails, it produced a brilliant ringing sound. The Gaelic harp (the historical *cláirseach* or Irish harp) was the highest status musical instrument of both Scotland and Ireland, and harpers were amongst the most prestigious cultural figures amongst Irish and Scottish kings and chiefs. In both countries, the harper enjoyed special rights and played a crucial part in ceremonial occasions such as coronation and poetic recital. The main function of the Gaelic harp in medieval

6. Ibid. p 546.
7. Ibid. p 693

Scotland and Ireland seems to have been playing to accompany the recitation of bardic poetry in Gaelic or Irish. At one point in Irish history, conquering invaders made it illegal to possess an Irish harp and set out to burn every harp in Ireland in an attempt to kill the 'Irish spirit'. From early times to the end of the nineteenth century, the harp was at the social centre of Ireland. The harpist, often blind, accompanied poets who sang the glory of their kings. Ireland is unique in having a musical instrument, the harp, as its national emblem. Up to at least the seventeenth century, harpists enjoyed a high status among all other musicians and in society. This second buttress to the Underground Cathedral restores the place that poetry and music have held, and should hold, in our country.

Apart from the spire of this cathedral and the bridges as flying buttresses over the river, a most impressive sacristy has emerged in the shape and design of the Francis Bacon Studio. John Edwards, heir to the estate of the artist Francis Bacon (1909-92), bequeathed his studio at Reece Mews, London, and its contents to the Hugh Lane Municipal Gallery of Modern Art above the Spire in Parnell Square, the Art Museum where the Hugh Lane collection was eventually housed. 'About that original hen. [A]n iceclad shiverer, merest of bantlings observed a cold fowl behaviourising strangely on that fatal midden or chip factory or comicalbottomed copsjute (dump for short) afterwards changed into the orangery when in the course of deeper demolition unexpectedly one bushman's holiday its limon threw up a few spontaneous fragments of orangepeel, the last remains of an outdoor meal by some unknown sunseeker or placehider illico way back in his mistridden past' [FW 110]. From 28 October 2009 until March 2010 an exhibition at this same Municipal Gallery takes place: *Francis Bacon: A Terrible Beauty* celebrates the centenary of Francis Bacon's birth in 63, Lower Baggot Street, Dublin in October 1909. This exhibition comprising paintings, drawings, photographs, unfinished works and slashed canvases, offers an astonishing new look at one of the great figurative painters of the twentieth century.

From the sacristy of the cathedral I was led into the crypt. Since 1998 Lorcan Walshe, a Dublin artist, has been resurrecting Celtic and pre Celtic artefacts, working in the National Museum at Collins Barracks for three months each year over a four year period. This National Museum of Ireland was opened in 1890 and was the result of the merging together of several Irish collections. It contains artefacts and masterpieces dating from 2000 BC to the twentieth century. The archaeological collections consist of the National Treasury (which includes the Ardagh Chalice, Tara Brooch and Cross of Cong), the Ór – Ireland's gold exhibition which features the finest collection of prehistoric gold artefacts in Europe. Viking Age Ireland, focuses on Irish Archaelogy from 800-1200 AD. 'What child of a strandlooper but keepy little Kevin in the despondful surrounding of such sneezing cold would ever have trouved up on a strate that was called strete a motive for future saintity by euchring the finding of the Ardagh chalice by another heily innocent and beachwalker whilst trying with pious clamour to wheedle Tipperaw raw raw reeraw puteters out of Now Sealand in spignt of the patchpurple of the massacre, a dual a duel to die to day, goddam and biggod, sticks and stanks, of most of the Jacobiters'[FW 111].[8]

The museum houses a collection of ancient objects as diverse as Bronze Age containers, Stone Age spirals, Medieval chalices, croziers, reliquaries, bells. Lorcan Walshe's art is a ritual whereby the spirit of these ancient objects is made present to us today. In his drawings he works past the surface detail and captures the essence of the artefacts and the sensibility of the craftsperson who created them. More than that, he shows that the original inspiration for such work was a religious one, that reverence is what imbued each craft with the artistic genius now incarnated in the objects themselves. Through his painstaking representation of the works themselves he can make manifest the aura which radiates from each artefact as a kind of phosphorescence. Yet, the manifestation occurs, not in the attempt to paint or to draw any such phosphorescence, but rather in attention to the exact representation of the object itself.

Such painstaking painterly stalking of the artefact is not just recording, in the sense that if the objects were stolen or if they were destroyed by fire or in an earthquake we would have a

---

8. James Joyce, *Finnegans Wake*, London, Faber, 1975. Hereafter referred to as FW with page number in square brackets.

representative file of what had been there. More than that, these entrapments of the Spirit, dream-catchers, make present in a real way the originality of the instruments or vessels. 'You should understand this as a monk,' Lorcan suggests to me, 'Artists of old believed that God would be encompassed within their works as in a tabernacle or a reliquary. What they may have failed to notice is that God was actually present in the making and that this presence is still inscribed in whatever they made.' Medieval artists and craftspeople believed that they were encircling and embossing a piece of the Divine inside the reliquaries and shrines they were fashioning. Sometimes one work of this kind took up a whole lifetime, maybe two lifetimes. Taking an arial view of the medieval forest shows a major shift in human consciousness similar to the one which occurred in chronological sequence throughout the first part of the twentieth century: the dialectic between figurative and abstract rendition. Within essentially functional art (all these croziers, vessels, reliquaries and bells were being used for a very specific purpose), appears a quality of abstraction. This medieval craftmanship is simultaneously representational and abstract and rides like an expert windsurfer the cusp of both. As Mainie Jellet says: 'If an Irish artist of the eighth or ninth century were to meet a present-day cubist or non-representational painter, they would understand each other.'[9]

The Irish Museum of Modern Art (IMMA), officially opened in May 1991, is housed in the Royal Hospital Kilmainham, one of the finest seventeenth-century buildings in Ireland. The Royal Hospital itself was founded in 1684 by James Butler, Duke of Ormonde and Viceroy to Charles II, as a home for retired soldiers, and continued in that use for almost 250 years. The style is based on Les Invalides in Paris with a formal facade and a large elegant courtyard. It was restored by the government in 1984.

Anne Madden had a retrospective exhibition of her paintings from 1950 to 2007 at the IMMA from June until September, 2007. This provided an aerial view of the Underground Cathedral plan with a stunning glimpse of light at the end of the

9. Jellet, 'A Word on Irish art,' in Eileen McCarvill's *The Artist's Vision*, Dundalgan Press, Dundalk, 1958, p 105.

tunnel. Here was half a century of perspicacious susceptivity on display. After the darkest century which the planet may ever have endured, her panoramic overview develops both the darkness and then the light and the colour as a pyrotechnic possibility of eventual emergence in her paintings of Aurora borealis.

People still go to art galleries to see objects, to recognise their own domestic animals parading. They do not understand that we should be going to art galleries not simply to see what we have already seen, what we recognise, what we already know; we also go there to see what the eye has not yet imagined and which comes towards us, not as something domesticated and familiar, but as an intense feeling that edges its way towards appearance. Seeing this exhibition changed my sensibility and, I think, has established a distinct and alternative intentionality for all of us at the beginning of this twenty-first century. 'It has been said that art is the child of its age. Such an art can only create an artistic feeling which is already clearly felt. This art, which has no power for the future, which is only a child of the age and cannot become a mother of the future, is a barren art. That which belongs to the spirit of the future can only be realised in feeling, and to this feeling the talent of the artist is the only road.'[10] Such an artist helps the evolutionary appetite of creation towards the goal for which it was intended. The whole sweep and movement of Anne Madden's life as displayed in this dramatic presentation is a very subtle and delicate invitation to *Westward Ho!* We are taken in a dance movement onwards and upwards. Art of the future has no template, no guide, no intellectual categories; it feels its way forward. And the exteriorisation of this inner feeling is colour. The artist pours out the feeling in colour which almost bleeds through onto the canvas and there seeps its way into shape and form. What belongs to the spirit of the future can only be realised in feeling, and to this feeling the talent of the artist is our most adequate guide.

Such art is spiritual work, the work of creating the future. Its major display case is colour. Colour is a power which directly influences the soul. Colour is the keyboard, the eyes are the

---

10. Wassily Kandinsky, *Concerning the Spiritual in Art*, Dover Publications, New York, 1977, p 25.

hammers, the soul is the piano with many strings. The artist is the hand which plays, touching one key or another, to cause vibrations in the soul.'[11]

Art galleries and theatres make up the nave and the transepts of the Underground Cathedral. The Abbey Theatre first opened its doors to the public on 27 December 1904, so it spans the twentieth century and parallels the life of the Irish State. Despite losing its original building to a fire in 1951, it has remained active to the present day. The Abbey was the first state-subsidised theatre in the English-speaking world; from 1925 onwards it received an annual subsidy from the Irish Free State. Since July 1966, it has been located at 26 Lower Abbey Street, Dublin. In its early years, it was closely associated with the writers of the Irish Literary Revival, many of whom were involved in its founding and most of whom had plays staged there. It has been from the beginning the narthex of the Underground Cathedral. Its companion, The Gate Theatre, was established in 1928 by Hilton Edwards and Micheál Mac-Liammóir. These offered Dublin audiences an introduction to the world of European and American avant-garde theatre as well as well as classics from the modern and Irish repertoire.

Marina Carr has infiltrated the Underground Cathedral and provided a Lady Chapel and marble for the wreathed columns. Her play *Woman and Scarecrow* focuses upon two great mysteries of the conscious and unconscious life, death and femininity. Expressionist plays often dramatised the spiritual awakening and sufferings of their protagonists, in such a way that they were referred to as *Stationendramen* (station plays). These were often modelled on the episodic presentation of the suffering and death of Jesus Christ in the Stations of the Cross. In such expressionist drama, the speech is heightened, whether expansive and rhapsodic, or clipped and telegraphic; it is a coded history of suffering which leads to resurrection. I saw this play in the Peacock Theatre on Thursday 18 October 2007, and then attended a public discussion of the play on Tuesday 30 October 2007 where many in the audience expressed their feelings that this play was for them the life of Christ with a woman acting as Jesus.

---

11. Ibid.

On Friday 6 March 2009 I had the opportunity of seeing Marina Carr's *The Giant Blue Hand*, at the Ark Cultural Centre for Children, directed by Selina Cartmell. It was a magic experience with all the children moving in and out of the Ark in serried rows of ecstatic hysteria. The plot centres on a huge, terrifying hand which steals away Mr and Mrs Time and their baby, Dilly, and holds them captive at the bottom of the ocean. It's up to two children to find and rescue them. 'Time can do terrible things,' says Queen Dalia, 'but it can also do the wonderful.' As nature imitating art, in April 2009, a giant blue hand was discovered crushing the stars in outer space. Nasa has produced a new image from their Chandra X-ray Observatory, depicting high-energy X-rays emanating from the nebula around the dying star, PSR B1509-58, as coloured blue to reveal a structure resembling a giant blue hand reaching for some eternal red cosmic light. Visible icons of the Giant Blue Hand which buries time as we record it consciously at the bottom of the sea of our unconscious. And in the closing scene of Carr's play, Don Wycherley begins to tell the story of *marmar* (the Irish for Marble), but, as he says, that's a tale for another time. So, I had to go to hear that other tale told at the Abbey Theatre in the narthex of the Underground Cathedral. 'Is not sleep perhaps the true home of the self, like the sea from which humankind first emerged at the dawn of time ...? But if that is so, how can we re-enter that other life and yet remain awake enough to know it?' (Gabriel Josipovici)

Marina's play *Marble*[12] suggests that we have at least two kinds of dream, that the unconscious reservoir is multilayered, and that at least one of those layers is available to the Holy Spirit. Dreams of this kind are marble dreams. Marble comes from the Greek μάρμαρον (*marmaron*), 'crystalline rock,' or 'shining stone' from the verb μαρμαίρω, 'to flash, sparkle, gleam.' One of the women in the play admits to: 'Polishing my white marble tiles in the hall. I'm in love with those tiles. I made Art import them. I love the sheen, the light, the texture and grain.'[13] The metamorphic process which turns ordinary stone into marble causes a complete recrystallisation of the original rock into an interlocking mosaic of crystals, so marble is different

12. Marina Carr, *Marble*, The Gallery Press, 2009
13. Ibid, p 51.

from all other kinds of rock. The reason for this is because the temperatures and pressures necessary to form marble usually destroy any fossils or sedimentary textures present in the original rock. So, the heat and the pressure of certain lives change us, transfigure us into a different species. Marble souls are like those indigo children with a different kind of psyche from the rest. Sedimentary rock, your ordinary everyday sedentary human, is formed by deposition and consolidation of mineral and organic material. Whatever happens naturally, the growth and fall of leaves etc, the diary entries of every normal tedious day, comprise 80% of all rock of earth's land area, and of us as the human population. Such rock formed from sediments is classified by the source from which these sediments come: such as limestone, chalk, sandstone; in our case: drink, sex and shopping, as described by Anne, one of the characters in Carr's play.

Marble is different. It somehow divests itself of the sediment, of the roots from which it is formed, and transforms itself into gossamer woven above the maelstrom of evolution. As the butterfly releases itself from the cocoon and flies off into the ether, so marble releases itself from the dross and dances into its own element. The characteristic swirls and veins of many coloured marble varieties are remnants of various (mineral) impurities which remain like scars from elements which have been cauterised or amputated such as clay, silt, sand, iron oxides or chert.

Dreams are like rocks also. There are sedimentary dreams and marble dreams. We are influenced by the Freudian theory of dreams, 'the guardians of sleep' which allow the hidden wishes of daytime to enter consciousness without shocking us sufficiently to wake us up. These wishes arrive in dreams as a code to be decoded, and are sufficiently disguised to prevent us from panicking into wakefulness. Freud was so convinced that his interpretation of dreams was 'the royal road to knowledge of the unconscious activities of the mind'[14] that, while he was on holiday in Belle Vue Castle near Vienna in 1895, he fantasised that some day – wait for it – 'a marble tablet' would record that 'in this house July 24th 1895, the Secret of dreams was revealed to Dr Sigmund Freud.'[15]

For Freud, dreams were like the 80% of sedimentary rock

14. *The Interpretation of Dreams*, Penguin Freud Library, 1991, p 769.
15. Anthony Stevens, *Jung: A Very Short Introduction*, OUP, 1994, p 103.

formed from memory residue: events from the previous day and from childhood. He made no allowance for those dreams of marble which eschew such mundane origins. Jung, on the other hand, maintained that dreams drew upon a deeper source belonging to the evolutionary history of our species, which he called the collective unconscious. 'Dreams always stress the other side in order to maintain the psychic equilibrium.'[16]

The Talmud tells us that the dream is its own interpretation. 'The whole dream-work is essentially subjective, and a dream is a theatre in which the dreamer is himself the scene, the player, the prompter, the producer, the author, the public and the critic.'[17] So, the theatre is the way to process certain deep dreams of a whole society – social dreaming. Marina Carr's play *Marble* is our society dreaming beyond 'the tender trap,' the socio-political norms which hold us in a vice-like grip.

As Anthony Storr comments: 'Whereas Freud held the purpose of the dream to be one of deception so as to outwit the censor and enable the shadow to enter consciousness in disguise, Jung thought its purpose was to serve individuation by making valuable unconscious potential available to the whole personality.' And, by extension, this play provides what Heaney calls the 'ameliorating effect of theatre ... which engages at serious imaginative levels with societies in crisis and transition.'[18]

My final example of the Underground Cathedral emerging in Ireland is the 2008 film *Garage* starring Pat Shortt, directed by Lenny Abrahamson and written by Mark O'Halloran. Set somewhere in Tipperary, on the edge of a sleepy village, we see Pat Shortt's simple-minded and kind-hearted Josie work in a small garage for a former classmate (John Keogh). The garage is located on one of the latter's dilapidated properties until the right offer comes and it will be sold to developers.

Regarded by his neighbours as a harmless misfit, Josie has spent all his adult life as caretaker of this crumbling garage. Pat Shortt's virtuoso performance aside, the great achievement here is an Irish film whose story could be transported to anywhere.

16. C. G. Jung, *Collected Works*, vii, para 170, Bollinger Series XX, 1966.
17. Ibid, viii, para 509.
18. Seamus Heaney, *Spelling It Out,* in honour of Brian Friel on his 80th birthday, Gallery Books, 9 January, 2009.

The setting is parochial, but the themes and emotions are universal. Ireland before the Celtic Tiger was that crumbling petrol station on the outskirts of Europe waiting for truck drivers from the EC to fill us up and we, as a nation, were the simple-minded and kind-hearted Josie so devastatingly portrayed by Pat Shortt.

And the call of the film was 'Horse' – my kingdom for a horse, and all that horse means for rural Ireland, ecology, economy and education and finally for one of the oldest mythologies on the planet – the underground where perhaps the better half of our humanity is also horse. For contemporary cultures no longer dependent on the horse for food, draught, or transportation, urban children become familiar with Horse mainly through folk and fairy tales, movies and television. For them, only a mythical relationship to horses exists.

Most folk tales portray Horse as an extension of the rider and an accessory to the Hero's quest. Horse is literally and figuratively a means of transport across the terrain of the tale's setting and into the internal landscape of the Hero's journey of self-discovery and awareness. In Egyptian, Greek, Armenian, Norse, and Hindu mythological traditions, horse pulls the sun (and sometimes the moon) across the sky. The Four Horsemen of the Apocalypse usher in the end of the world, the second coming of the Messiah. Muhammad, Vishnu, and Christ are all prophesied to return on a white horse.

Late palaeolithic human beings hunted wild horses for food, evidently used them also in ritual ceremonies, and vividly depicted them in cave art found all over Europe and Asia Minor. Examples are the Lascaux cave artists. Both Vedic and Celtic myths relate the deeper significance of mating with the horse, not just as a fertility rite, but as union with the Divine. T. C. Lethbridge describes a ritual, which he personally witnessed in Ireland in the seventeenth century, where the king physically mates with a mare in an enactment of union with the Divine Sovereign Goddess. In this Ulster ritual, the mare is also divided into three parts, which are boiled to form a broth in which the king bathes and which are then consumed. The horse calls out to Josie from the Underground Cathedral and gallops to meet him as he reaches the shore. Our primary task at present is to establish contact with this other half of ourselves.

## CHAPTER THIRTEEN

# The Gospel According to Thomas

*The Gospel of Thomas* is a New Testament-era apocryphon, almost completely preserved in a Coptic papyrus manuscript discovered in 1945 at Nag Hammadi in Egypt, ten years after Tom Murphy was born. The writer is styled Didymus (Greek = Twin) Judas (rendering of the Hebrew name *Yehudah*, Hebrew: הָדּוּהְי), Thomas (Hebrew = Twin). Early Christian communities clustered around various disciples of Jesus but only a few remain as recognised templates for contemporary Christians. Certain passages in the gospel of John can only be understood in light of a community based on the theological teachings of the gospel of Thomas. John is the only one of the canonical gospels that gives Thomas a speaking part – indicating respect for the Thomas community. This is because the gospel of John and the gospel of Thomas are theologically similar in almost every respect except one. In the story of 'Doubting Thomas' the Johannine Community is theologically rebutting the Thomas Community. The Johannine Community believes in a bodily resurrection; the Thomas community believes in a spiritual resurrection — and completely rejects a bodily one. So the gospel of John has Thomas physically touch the risen Jesus and acknowledge his bodily nature.

No major Christian group accepts this Thomas gospel as canonical or authoritative. In the fourth century Cyril of Jerusalem wrote, 'Let none read the gospel according to Thomas: for it is the work not of one of the twelve apostles, but of one of the three wicked disciples of Manes.' The fifth-century *Decretum Gelasanium*: calls it 'a gospel attributed to Thomas which the Manichaeans use,' and lists it as heretical. So we are back to the Manichaean heresy, the one that divides the world into two warring principles, where the body, the flesh, sexuality are on the evil side of the divide. The Catholicism that twentieth century Ireland taught her children was of this variety. Tom Murphy embraced this version of Catholicism wholeheartedly as a boy and later repudiated, it rewriting its 'Gospel' in his plays.

'Once upon a time there was a boy … and he was given a dream, his life (and) … And the church told him of God, kind God and guardian angels. And how everyone is made just like God – even the little boy himself was. (…) Yes, everyone gave the little boy balloons, the most expensive balloons, already inflated, yellow, green, blue and red, the very best of colours, and they floated above him, nodding and bobbing, and lifting his feet clear off the ground so that he never had to walk a step anywhere. Until one day, one of them burst, and it was the beautiful blue one. And he was not prepared for this. So, one day he walked away into the forest forever.'[1]

Tom Murphy growing up in Tuam, Co Galway, according to himself, 'believed totally and implicitly in the fairytale of religion.' John McGahern describes a similar experience and explains how so many young people in Ireland at that time chose the religious life or priesthood as their avocation:

All through this schooling there was the pressure to enter the priesthood, not from the decent Brothers but from within oneself. The whole of our general idea of life still came from the church, clouded by all kinds of adolescent emotions heightened by the sacraments and prayers and ceremonies. Still at the centre was the idea: in my end is my beginning. The attraction was not joy or the joyous altar of God; it was dark, ominous, and mysterious, as befits adolescence and the taking up, voluntarily, of our future death at the very beginning of life, as if sacrificing it to a feared God in order to avert future retribution. There was, too, the comfort of giving all the turmoil and confusion of adolescence into the safekeeping of an idea.[2]

Born in 1935, Tom Murphy embraced fanatically and uncompromisingly the world of the Medieval Cathedral which was presented to him and which he absorbed wholeheartedly.

---

1. Tom Murphy, *The Morning after Optimism*, London, Methuen Drama, 2001, p 40.
2. John McGahern, *Love of the World*, Faber, London, 2009, p 142.

He quotes James Agee, *The Morning Watch* (1951) as the book which most accurately represents his childhood religion. Like many other young people growing up in Ireland in the middle of the last century he was bewitched by the lifestyle presented to him in the Catholic ideal taught by his family and those educating him. 'I enjoyed them, or I enjoyed them in retrospect. The dressing-up, the drag, the candles, the incense, the singing, the choirs and the dark sound of Latin has fed me and fed my work through the years.' He traces the anger which most people detect in his plays to the 'betrayal of having been fed so many false dreams' by 'extremely naïve and ignorant men'.[3]

John McGahern, a year older than Tom Murphy, records similar impressions: 'There were the great ceremonies of Christmas and Easter, but the ceremonies I remember best are the stations of the cross in Lent and the Corpus Christi processions. There were never more than a handful of people present at these Lenten Stations gathered beneath the organ loft. In the dimly lit church, rain and wind often beating at the windows, the church smelling of damp, the surpliced priest, three altar boys in scarlet and white, one with a cross in front, two bearing lighted candles, moved from station to station, the name of each echoing in the nearly empty church, "Veronica Wipes the Face of Jesus", along with the prayer, "O Jesus who for love of me didst bear Thy cross;/To Calvary in Thy sweet mercy grant to me to suffer;/And to die with Thee", chanted at each station.'

> Corpus Christi was summer. Rhododendron and lilac branches were taken by cart and small tractors from the Oakport Woods and used to decorate the grass margins of the triangular field around the village. Coloured streamers and banners were strung across the road from poles. Altars with flowers and a cross on white linen were erected at Gilligan's, the post office and at Mrs Mullaney's. The host was taken from the tabernacle and carried by the priests beneath a gold canopy all the way round the village, pausing for ceremonies at each wayside altar. Benediction was always at the post office. The congregation followed behind,

---

3. *Reading the Future, Irish Writers in Conversation with Mike Murphy*, ed Clíodhna Ní Anluain, Lilliput, Dublin, 2000, p 177.

some bearing the banners of their sodalities, and girls in white veils and dresses scattered rose petals from white boxes on the path before the host.[4]

Murphy fell prey as a young person to what he calls 'The Seduction of Morality' which later became a novel and a play about life in Tuam. There is a huge attraction about the ideal of purity which the Catholic Church was purveying and incarnating in the island of Ireland at that time. Murphy's eldest brother left home in 1939 when Tom was four. 'He became a strange, almost mythical, figure in my life. He married, divorced and married again, so he was excommunicated, not officially, but he might as well have been with the whispering in the house at night between my mother and my sisters and brothers about this poor lost sheep. I prayed and prayed that I would one day find him and bring him home and take him to the parish priest, who would somehow or other save his soul before he died.' There was huge resentment and anger in Murphy and in his work because that kind of 'stuff' was inflicted on him and on his family. All his later life was *The Morning After Optimism*, and he set about the task of being Devil's Advocate to the humanity which twentieth century Ireland seemed determined to canonise.

In 1970 the International Commission on English in the Liturgy met in Dublin and attended a play at the Abbey by Murphy called *A Crucial Week in the Life of a Grocer's Assistant*. They were so impressed that they asked Tom Murphy to help them with their work of translating all the rites, sacraments, and services of the Catholic Church into English, following the desire of Vatican II to use vernacular languages. Murphy became one of the Commission's twelve members, ten of whom were priests. At meetings in Rome, Washington and Toronto, he helped to shape the prayers which millions of Catholics around the world utter every day. He told the priest who commissioned him that he was not a Catholic and would not wish Catholicism as he had known it on anyone. However, he absorbed himself in the language of religion without bringing back to himself the faith of his childhood. 'I retired from that after two years because it was wrong for me to be trying to fashion prayers for

---

4. John McGahern, *Love of the World*, p 138.

other people that I didn't believe in myself. I found I was further removed from the God of my childhood. This was two years before I wrote *The Sanctuary Lamp*.'[5] 'He was shaping things for others in which he did not himself believe. He found that there was no salvation in the church. Having failed to transform the old religion to his satisfaction, he went on to imaginatively create a new one.'[6] The theatre of Tom Murphy has been spoken of as a holy theatre, a search for soul in a soulless world, a theatre of the possible, a theatre of the spirit. His language is a search for images, symbols and myths that will enable us to tell the story of who we are.

The sanctuary lamp has been a central Judaeo-Christian symbol for at least 3,500 years. And in the last thirty-five years this haunting, brooding, silent, yet endearing presence has been even more poignantly alive since Tom Murphy's dramatic representation of it. In Hebrew, *ner tamid* (דימת רנ), means 'eternal flame.' The Pentateuch prescribes that such a lamp 'filled with the purest oil of olives' burn forever and always in the Tabernacle of the Lord, representing the Menorah of the Temple in Jerusalem, symbolising God's eternal presence. More locally, and particularly for Tom Murphy's Ireland, a conspicuous sanctuary lamp would have burned in every Roman Catholic church in the country, four years before the visit of Pope John Paul II, when its influence was high and mighty. 'In accordance with traditional custom, the Roman Missal prescribes a special lamp, fuelled by oil or wax, should be kept alight near the tabernacle to indicate and honour the presence of Christ.' Such sanctuary lamps were primary symbols of Irish Catholic identity in the culture and mentality of Tom Murphy's childhood. They were a particularly sensitive target for the kind of surgical probing with which his theatre is engaged.

*The Sanctuary Lamp* was first written in 1975 and revisited twenty-five years later at the beginning of the new millennium: a quarter of a century of spilt ink and boiling oil. Its first production was greeted with opproprium worthy of traditional

---

5. *Reading the Future*, p 180.
6. Fintan O'Toole, *The Politics of Magic, The Work and Times of Tom Murphy*, Raven Arts Press, Dublin, 1987, p. 144.

Abbey audiences. Salomes of every denomination danced for the head of Tom the Blasphemer. Cearbhall Ó Dálaigh, then President of Ireland, saw beyond the 'thundering disgrace' and declared the play to be one of the great achievements of the Abbey Theatre since *The Playboy of the Western World* and *Juno and the Paycock*. Certainly, if success is to be measured by the noisy rejection meted out to *The Playboy* and *The Plough and the Stars*, then this play must be counted among the greats. The trauma of such rejection caused Tom Murphy to withdraw from writing plays for a number of years.

What early audiences understood as anti-Catholic tongue-lashing, shows itself today, in the light of later history, as prophetic admonition about spiritual hype and institutional hypocrisy. Our theology was, perhaps, too simplistic and self-congratulatory to weather the oncoming storms and consequent vandalism of the sanctuary. 'In the last scene ... the ritual of replacing the candle in the sanctuary lamp suggests a re-conception of the Christian religion of love, freed of its church institutionalisation.'[7] Judeo-Christianity is too subtle and too great a mystery to be left to formulaic pieties of self-righteous believers. The mystery of God's presence is more than everything that can be said about it, and certainly more than Irish Catholics were led to believe in the first half of the twentieth century. *The Sanctuary Lamp* stands as eloquent testimony to a presence which belongs to all of us, Jews, Christians and Gentiles alike, a lamp burning in the heart of each one of us, but beyond the reach of any, or all.

Essentially this is theatre where presence is ontological and eternal. This is no time for politics or preaching. Murphy rails against the institutional church but celebrates the spiritual one. And the play itself is homage to the architectural church, showing respect for its dark heights and recesses, for the physical and artistic legacy of Christianity.

Three weary travellers seek sanctuary overnight in a church. Harry, the English-born Jew and ex-circus strongman, praying to the flickering candle in the sanctuary lamp for strength to kill

---

7. Nicholas Grene, 'Voice and Violence in Murphy' in *Alive in Time, The Enduring Drama of Tom Murphy: New Essays*, ed Christopher Murray, Dublin, Carysfort Press, 2010, p. 36.

his wife and his best friend. Maudie, sixteen year old runaway waif, haunted by her past waiting for the release of forgiveness. Irish blackguard, Francisco, who doesn't want anything. They are alien to the church's creed, and have little or no respect for its rituals and liturgy. Their actions are superficially profane – violence, swearing, sexual innuendo, drunkenness. But their accounts of themselves are confessional, and their purpose in being there is true to the essence of the church of the crucifixion: the confronting of despair. Francisco proclaims an alternative Christianity from the pulpit:

> 'I have a dream, I have a dream! The day is coming, the second coming, the final judgement, the not too distant future, before that simple light of man: when Jesus, Man, total man, will call to his side the goats – "Come ye blessed!" Yea, call to his side all those rakish, dissolute, suicidal, fornicating goats, taken in adultery and what-have-you. And proclaim to the coonics, blush for shame, you blackguards, be off with you, you wretches, depart from me ye accursed complicated affliction! And that, my dear brother and sister, is my dream, my hope, my vision and my belief.'[8]

The Gospel of Thomas Murphy? A resurrection of humankind as it is; a new translation of Christianity where the full spectrum of human complexity is what God came on earth to transfigure.

Csilla Bertha sees *The Sanctuary Lamp* as what she calls 'rituals of a lost faith.'

> The 'half-lapsed Jew' Harry and the 'self-destructive' ex-Jesuit Francisco may defy God, commit all sorts of sacrilege, may even have murderous intentions, yet at the end they do arrive at forgiveness under the 'Presence,' indicated by the sanctuary lamp, partaking in the sacraments through drinking of the altar wine and sharing bread and fish and finally, joining together in the confessional box. The mystery of the play lies in the manner Murphy uses the sacred place and objects together with scraps of the liturgical structure and language so that everything lends itself to a reading of a renouncing of Christianity but, at the same time also to that

---

8. Tom Murphy, *The Sanctuary Lamp*, Methuen Drama, London, 2001, p 58.

of an embracing of a faith in divinely animated interhuman relations.[9]

She even makes a plausible argument for *The Sanctuary Lamp* as a Post-Modern, Post-Christian, rediscovery of God 'after God' in the vein of Richard Kearney's religion of 'Anatheism.'[10] She claims that 'although Murphy's deviation from conventional Catholicism is clear in all his work, his dramatic world's rootedness in Christianity remains equally clear, however unorthodox and undogmatic it may be.'[11]

In 1983 Tom Murphy dramatized the new Ireland of prosperous business tycoons and middle-class suburban affluence and ennui. *The Gigli Concert* is a searching, challenging and funny play dealing with seven days in the relationship between Dynamatologist J. P. W. King, a quack self-help therapist living in Dublin, but born and brought up in England, and the mysterious Irishman, a despairing property magnate who seeks out King to help him sing like the great Italian opera singer Beniamino Gigli. In the course of the play, the depressed Irish property developer has five manic 'consultations' with the English dynamatologist. The Irishman is the archetypal business success of the sixties, a builder and property developer. He could be Harry from *A Whistle in the Dark* twenty years on. A self-made man, he has spent most of his time and energy getting his two million into the bank. But now he is dissatisfied. He has a wife and child but the would-be bliss of domesticity frustrates him to violence and obscenity. He wants something more than this. He articulates his desire as wanting to sing like the Italian tenor Beniamino Gigli. He has selected Mr J. P. W. King to help him make this happen.

This play can also support the argument proposed by Bertha especially, as she also points out, when in the introduction to

---

9. Csilla Bertha, '"Rituals of a Lost Faith"?: Murphy's Theatre of the Possible,' in *Alive in Time, The Enduring Drama of Tom Murphy: New Essays*, ed Christopher Murray, Dublin, Carysfort Press, 2010, p 278.
10. Richard Kearney, *Anatheism* {Returning to God after God} New York, Columbia University Press, 2010.
11. Csilla Bertha, '"Rituals of a Lost Faith"?: Murphy's Theatre of the Possible,' in *Alive in Time, The Enduring Drama of Tom Murphy: New Essays*, ed Christopher Murray, Dublin, Carysfort Press, 2010, p 275.

Kearney's Hermeneutics of Religion, *The God Who May Be*, he explicitly names Murphy as a source for 'the kind of philosophy of God' which he is proposing: 'The neologism, *dynamatology*, first came to me in conversation with ... Tom Murphy in the early eighties in Dublin when we were discussing some ideas for a new play he was working on, *The Gigli Concert*. In it there is a character who wants to teach people to "sing like Gigli," the great genius of Italian opera, thereby inviting them to come into contact with their innermost potential. The term Murphy and I hit upon to convey the meaning of this "logic of the dynamizing possible" was dynamatology. There was of course a certain ludic poetic license to this coinage which perhaps renders it more suited to theatre than to philosophy in the strict sense. But then maybe philosophy needs a little poetics betimes.'[12]

Murphy contacted Patrick Mason to see if he would be interested in directing the first production in 1983. Mason had read the play and when Murphy asked him what he thought it was about he said: 'the song of the soul in a contemporary world,' which, according to Mason, was satisfactory enough for Murphy to want to work with him. 'You don't need to know the words: hear the sounds,' advises the 'dynamatologist', in his attempt to help the burnt-out Irish property developer. 'I had wanted to write something about singing,' Murphy recalls. 'I've never been envious of any other playwright but I got to the point where I actually couldn't bear to listen to singers because I so envied the expressive power that music can possess.'[13]

'I thought of this character who has this impossible, crazy, ambition to sing like Gigli,' he says. 'I chose Gigli because he had a very pure voice, even in his late sixties he could produce this incredibly pure sound. I thought it was a sound that could be both haunting and crucifying to someone like the Irishman who has sold out, so we get this picture of the human spirit in both joy and pain.'

'I've been told my characters tend to be harsh but if that's so,

12. Richard Kearney, *The God Who May Be*, Indiana University Press, 2001, p 6.
13. Charlie McBride, Tom Murphy – Conversations on the Gigli Concert, *The Galway Advertiser*, 25 June 2009.

the harshness is only there because they feel they have been betrayed somehow or that they have betrayed something in themselves. The music is like a cry or an echo of that.'

Irish Catholicism presented an idyllic existence for the boy soprano whose voice has not yet broken. Its world of pre-pubertal purity comes crashing down when the *wunderkind* finds that his voice no longer holds the crowds in thrall. The songbird has become a very ordinary crow. Being a child soprano is one thing; living out the rest of your life is quite another. 'The Irish man is fixated on Gigli, he has read his memoir and he presents details from that as though it were his life, he is trying to live out that obsession. J. P. W. meanwhile fantasises about the absent woman Helen. Mona meanwhile has invented a godchild that she pretends to have taken to different places.'[14]

Murphy spoke of his play to Mike Murphy in the year 2000: 'I heard as recently as last week, coming from RTÉ radio, people discussing God's gender and I thought, "Have we moved on at all?", that this really bad fairytale is still being peddled. "God, is it a He? Is it a She? Is it a bird?" I find I get angry about that. I think that nature is God. I think that we are God. Indeed, I've written about this in *The Gigli Concert*: "God created the world, in order to create himself." We are God.'[15]

---

14. Ibid.
15. *Reading the Future*, p 178.

# CHAPTER FOURTEEN

## *September, October, November*

As if to prove the point of our obtuse repetitive slavery to tradition, our failure to express our own values and create our own culture, we can examine our twenty-first century diaries. In our Western world, we derive our calendar from the Romans. We begin each year on 1 January, named after Janus, the God of gateways, whose festival was celebrated by the Romans at that time of year. July and August are called after Julius Caesar and his successor Caesar Augustus. We even accept that these months should have thirty-one days because Augustus decided to lengthen his lest it be shorter than his predecessor's. To redress the imbalance, he also decreed that February have twenty-eight days. Amazing that these time-shares have survived. You would imagine that our more recent puritanical ancestors would have run a mile from such paganism. But, in truth, running a mile was also a Roman invention. It was the Latin for a thousand and measured a thousand paces. Only at the end of the twentieth century did we take to running in metres.

September, October, November are the Latin for seven to ten, *septem, octo, novem*. Until about 150 BC, the Roman year began in March. So, these last months were the seventh, eighth, and ninth months after the beginning of the year in March. March was the beginning because Mars was the God of war. Each year we were going into battle. We are living our battle in a carefully constructed world encased in a Roman time-machine. The battle between art and ideology involved many admirable warriors in various different fields. I have chosen three to represent the struggle in painting, drama, and poetry, their birthdays, which were celebrated in the early years of this century, ninety, eighty and seventy, respectively, describe the length of their struggle with the twentieth century.

NOVEMBER: LOUIS LE BROCQUY AND THE NUCLEAR FAMILY

Louis le Brocquy's ninetieth birthday was on 10 November 2006. Louis and the Irish Republic are the same age. It was in April of the year in which Louis was born, while the Great War was in the balance and the Battle of the Somme was raging, that the 1916 Rising occurred and the Proclamation of an Irish Republic was first made.

Roger Casement, who was hanged in that same year, declared before his death: 'Where all your rights become only an accumulated wrong; where people must beg with bated breath for leave to subsist in their own land … then surely it is a braver, a saner and a truer thing to be a rebel than tamely to accept it as the natural lot of men and women.'

Louis le Brocquy has been a rebel all his life. He has rebelled against the blindness which has been an affliction of his people and which he has refused to accept as their natural lot. He was born a seer among the visually impaired. Artists such as W. B. Yeats and Bernard Shaw protested vehemently at the passing of the Censorship Act 1929, and did manage to have the definition of 'indecent' as 'calculated to incite sexual passion' removed when they pointed out that this definition would deny Irish people access to most of the world's great art, whether secular or religious. However, the act went through and by 1930 every nude had been removed even from the Municipal Gallery, Ireland's show-case of 'modern' art at that time. Few artists felt welcome to express themselves in any but the most traditional fashion.

This did not mean however that in the early years of the twentieth century many Irish artists did not dedicate themselves to the project of imagining and thus creating a nation. Some put their art at the service of the newly established state and were content to portray the socio-political ideology of those in charge, others were less prepared to sacrifice their originality to such pre-cast structures.

For various reasons there was little promotion of art in Ireland at any level in the new dispensation. Art seemed to be, at the time, a luxury we could ill afford. As late even as 1961 a Scandinavian report on Design in Ireland stated that: 'The Irish schoolchild is visually and artistically among the most under-educated in Europe,' an indictment reechoed in 1965 by The Irish Council of Design which described education in this country as 'a tradition in which art as a whole has been gravely under-valued'. Over ten years later, after welcome reforms had been introduced into the education system, a report commissioned by The Arts Council of Ireland recognised that the 1970s were years of enlightened reform at every other level of the education sys-tem but 'the peripheral role which the arts have traditionally played in Irish Education has been perpetuated in the recent changes.' The same report warned that 'Ireland may be faced with a future public which, far from fruitfully exploiting the op-portunities available to it, may be characterised by a uniform mediocrity of taste controlled by commercial interests'.[1]

It was not until 1943 that Mainie Jellet, with Evie Hone and some others, founded the Irish Exhibition of Living Art, where it was possible to display work other than that which had been ap-proved by the 'founding fathers,' and to introduce into Ireland the revolution in painting which had been energising the rest of the world for over half a century. Initially a *salon des refusés*, this was to become a regular, and highly influential event. Their un-conventional step was taken partly out of frustration with the the Royal Hibernian Academy which was rejecting works of cer-tain contemporary artists for its prestigious exhibitions.

Change has indeed taken place, but only because of the work of certain rebellious geniuses like Louis le Brocquy. We have now in the National Gallery in Dublin his *A Family* which was painted in 1951, and which can act as symbol of the struggle be-tween art and officialdom over the half centuries which preceded and which followed its arrival on the scene. *A Family* has been recognised now as a seminal painting in the history of twentieth-century Irish art. Not only is it an important transitional move in le Brocquy's own work but one which anticipates 'modernism as an everyday style in Irish art.' This was exactly the kind of 'family' which we were desperately trying to keep out of Ireland, which we were saying had no part in the 'holy' family which our new nation was here to produce and to maintain. The

1. Ciarán Benson, *The Place of the Arts in Irish Education*, Report of the Arts Council's Working Party on the Arts in Education, 1979.

story of how it was first rejected and finally, fifty years later, installed as the only work of a living artist in the new Millennium Wing of the National Gallery of Ireland, recapitulates the struggle between Ireland and art in the twentieth century.

In the first year of this new millennium this painting cost £1.7 million sterling (US$ 2.4 m / €2.75 m) which underlines, in the only language the world at large really understands, Le Brocquy's importance in the pantheon of artists, setting a new record valuation for an Irish living artist. In 1952, when the painting was first offered to the Municipal Gallery of Modern Art in Dublin, 'to keep it in the country', by an interested group of art patrons it was going for £400. The gift was refused by the advisory committee of Dublin Corporation. It was famously described at the time as 'an unwholesome and satanic distortion of natural beauty.'[2] The decision to reject it did spark widespread controversy and extensive media coverage. Protests were led by the artists Norah McGuiness and Anne Yeats, but the decision stood. Instead the picture was sent for exhibition at the 1956 Venice *Biennale*, where it was awarded the prize, *Premio Acquisito Internationale*, and purchased by the Nestlé Corporation for their headquarters in Milan where it hung until 2001.

Le Brocquy, now so much part of the international arts establishment, was at the time something of a controversial figure, his work derided by fellow Irish artists, critics, journalists and correspondents to the letters columns. He himself recalls hearing people mocking even Jack Yeats' shows. Yeats had been known in the early part of the century as an exceptional painter of traditional Irish life. But 'just when he seemed in position to glory in his reputation as a great national painter, he found himself spurred on to paint as if he had no country at all: he had himself, and almost overnight, an unthinkable universe.' It was this 'unthinkable universe' that artists were trying to show us instead of the cosy pictures of 'traditional' Irish life which we were being encouraged to promote. Jack Yeats was one of the few people in Ireland who realised what contemporary physics was saying about the world we live in, and from 1925 he himself, as an artist, took a mid-life quantum leap into the new universe which science was now demonstrating. From that date

2. Letter to the *Irish Times* from 'Verdad' of Co Dublin, 6 March 1952.

onwards he began to paint physics: making visible to his contemporaries the new discoveries that 'molecules are more gap
than mass, more force than particle'. Yeats was aware of his important moment 'in the historical development of painting and
its relationship to particle physics.' He was one of the few who
were able to see, even in the myopically cloistered Ireland of his
day, the old world that had been blown to pieces and the new
one which we had been allowed to glimpse through the contemporary discoveries in science, especially particle physics.
'Without seeming to have theorised it in any depth (he despised
theories of painting) he gave it back as art.'[3] It was as if Yeats
had donned glasses that let him see, made him see, every visible
thing almost microscopically '... (and) to feel the underlying
movements of matter that are hidden from sight.'[4]

   Medical science announced in the year of Louis le Brocquy's
birth the discovery of a procedure by which internal organs
could be photographed. They called this discovery the X-ray.
Louis le Brocquy, probably from birth, was gifted with innate X-
ray vision. In a way comparable to Jack Yeats, he saw inner
being where others saw only a smiling face. Seamus Heaney
describes having his portrait painted by Louis as being 'le
Brocquified'. These are not simply portraits, they are images
towards a definition of the depths of human being, 'the spirit
within the reconstituted ancestral head,' the mystery of the person, 'lineaments of a plummet-measured face.' 'While his paintings are always seen to be concerned with the head image,'
Dorothy Walker points out with characteristic punctiliousness,
'he never paints the head but only the face.' Le Brocquy's vision
went inwards in the way that Jack Yeats' went outwards. One of
the people who influenced le Brocquy's vision was Erwin
Schrödinger (1887-1961), the Austrian Theoretical Physicist
whose contributions towards quantum mechanics, especially
the Schrödinger equation, won him the Nobel Prize in 1933. He
was in Dublin in 1942 and suggested that 'consciousness is a singular of which the plural is unknown and what appears to be
plurality is merely a series of different aspects of this one thing.'

3. Calvin Bedient, *The Yeats Brothers and Modernism's Love of Motion*,
University of Notre Dame Press, Indiana, 2009.
4. Ibid p 16.

This notion 'of an autonomous, disseminated consciousness surpassing individual personality' is akin to the theological possibility of the Holy Spirit and the mystery of our personality beyond personhood in the communion of saints. Whatever the verbal description, le Brocquy painted his search for this consciousness within all the heads that became his hall mark.

Both he and Jack Yeats certainly lived visually in an alternative world to the one being preached in the Ireland of their time. 'Looking back I can see that my work has always been concerned, in one way or another, with this inner consciousness which is, I imagine, our most profound reality. It is of course not possible to paint a concrete image of what is impalpable, but it would seem that my life as a painter has been largely spent in reaching towards an image implying its existence.'

An image implying the existence of what is impalpable, such has been his detective work of over a lifetime of art. When Brendan Kennelly had his experience of God after his heart operation in 1996 and wrote a poem about it called *The Man Made of Rain*, published in 1998, he used as a visual image on the front cover, le Brocquy's 1962 painting, *Isolated Being*, as illustration.

Le Brocquy recalled conversations at the time with 'people like Seán Keating who were naturally enough and, perhaps very properly, fearful and resentful of my kind of painting'.

Seán Keating, who was employed to paint the progress of the Shannon Hydro-Electric Scheme for instance, was illustrating the kind of Ireland which ideologues found pleasing, and 'his heroic narratives of the Irish and especially of the Western countrymen and women functioned to create a particular Irish national identity.'[5] Keating, whose pictures *Men of the South* and *Men of the West* had apotheosed Irish freedom fighters, continued his opposition to modern art right up to the late 1960s when he was filmed dismissing the works in the first *Rosc* exhibition. The world had moved on, and Keating's performance in the 1960s was amusing, but when in 1951 the older painter saw Le Brocquy's stark picture, *A Family*, he was one of the main people instrumental in its rejection by Dublin's Municipal Gallery. 'On the grounds of incompetence and of being offensive,' Le Brocquy said. 'I understood Seán Keating's concern at that time.

5. Ciarán Benson, *Studies*, Spring 1992, p 25.

That he could perceive this painting as a real threat to his own academic values.'

Keating was president of the RHA from 1951 to 1962. He did believe that the artist was a seer, but in the old Romantic notion displayed in his 1928-29 *Night's candles are Burnt out*, where 'only the artist and his wife are depicted as looking towards the future, in the form of the hydro-electric dam, and pointing it out to their children, the oncoming generation. None of the other six depicted adult figures looks to the future.'[6] Keating became 'whether positively or negatively, firmly placed in the public conscience as the artist that best exemplified the "Irishness" of "Irish Art".'[7] When the International Labour Offices in Geneva wanted an artistic contribution from Ireland, the Irish government awarded the commission to Keating. The theme was the development of labour in Ireland. The mural is still in place on the main stairway of the building which is now the World Trade Organisation.

But Ireland too has come of age visually, thanks to the foresight and hard work of many gifted artists, teachers and philanthropists. In a sale brokered by Mark Adams of the London art-dealers Agnew's, *A Family*[8] was acquired by Lochlann Quinn, Chairman of the AIB, and donated to the National Gallery, under the Irish government's scheme for tax relief on donations of objects of historical and cultural pre-eminence. The picture is displayed in the gallery's Millennium Wing, opened in January 2002, for which Louis le Brocquy also designed a monumental tapestry. As Medb Ruane has pointed out, 'the prophet has finally been honoured in his own land.'

'My own painting *A Family* was conceived in 1950 in very different circumstances in face of the atomic threat, social upheaval and refugees of World War II and its aftermath. Fifty years ago it was painted while contemplating a human condition stripped back to palaeolithic circumstance under the electric light bulbs,' the artist comments. 'One of our pleasures and

6. Ibid, p 26.
7. Eimear O'Connor, *Seán Keating in Context*, Carysfort Press, Dublin, 2009, p 63.
8. Dr Síghle Bhreathnach-Lynch, Curator of Irish Art at the National Gallery of Ireland, Dublin: 'An oil on canvas, almost two metres wide

one of our difficulties in relation to artists,' Anne Crookshank reminds us, 'is that they are in their very nature ahead and beyond us in thought and feeling.' How far ahead of us is summed up in an opinion published in a letter to the *Dublin Evening Mail*, 20 March 1952: 'There is a place for monstrosities in the College of Surgeons – there are plenty there – and it would give me much pleasure to find a place for things like 'The Family' [*sic*] ... It is not given to man to see into the future, but I am quite certain that in another 100 years the works of Turner, Constable, and a galaxy of true artists, whose work is still with us, will be cherished and admired, while things like 'The Family' [*sic*] will have returned to the oblivion from which they never should have emerged.'

There were some supporters of Le Brocquy at the time, including John Ryan, writing in *Our Nation* in January 1952: 'Louis le Brocquy discovered his peculiarly individual mode of expression early in his career and courageously employed it even when doing so meant that he had to discard a style which promised a fashionable and lucrative future as a portrait painter in the traditional manner. That pedestrian opinion has not forgiven him for this revolt against its standards was amply proved by the deplorable attack on the painter in the *Evening Herald* recently. Le Brocquy's stand and his subsequent development as an artist, however, won him the admiration and respect of intelligent opinion wherever his work has been shown.' John Ryan knew precisely how capable le Brocquy was of doing the kind of portraiture which would have won him favour and fortune, as he had painted a stunning portrait in the more conventional style, *Girl in White*, of Ryan's sister, Kathleen, a famous Hollywood actress at the time.

'Art is a secret logic of the imagination. This logic subverts actual worlds in the name of possible worlds. Reality is that

---

the picture depicts a family group ... The mother, lying on a table, leaning on one arm, stares out with quiet dignity while a menacing looking cat peers out from beneath the drawn sheet. In the background the father sits, head bowed, in a pose suggesting total dejection. He appears to be oblivious to the small child holding a bunch of flowers; a symbol of hope. The three sombrely painted figures inhabit a grey concrete bunker, lit by a bare bulb.'

which is possible not merely that which is happening around us. Art betrays itself when it subscribes to cultural insularism. Although the flowering of our imagination is nourished by roots hidden in our native soil, this flower is always shy of manipulative self-righteous national identity. Art keeps us dissatisfied with the established order of things. Le Brocquy's art reinterprets our everyday way of seeing. It is an uncompromising indictment of the perceptual, and by implication social, *status quo*. The present world of domination can never fully eliminate the potential world of freedom. "I often think of painting as being a kind of personal archaeology, I feel one is digging for things and suddenly something turns up which seems remarkable; something apparently outside oneself, which one has found in fact within oneself".'[9]

The former record for le Brocquy's work was £1.1 million sterling (US$ 1.6 m / €1.9 m) established at Sotheby's Irish Sale in 2000 for his painting *Tinker Woman with Newspaper*, from 1948. Le Brocquy's paintings of the 1940s are not some condescending or quaint studies of oddities from Irish society. His art is 'to penetrate actuality, to find in it a meaning'. The artist's task is to reveal the human in the human to the human 'because I am a human being myself'. In the 1940s Irish itinerants were the most colourful and obvious counterparts of artists themselves in Ireland, displaying 'fierce independence in a contemporary hostile world.'

Le Brocquy's later work, his studies towards a manifestation of W. B. Yeats, Joyce, Bacon, Beckett, Shakespeare, are, what he calls, archeological digs into their consciousness. He is revealing the divine face which is the fundamental reality of who we are at our most creative and at our most personal. He is showing Christ in the great artists of our tradition, our underground cathedral, as 'an autonomous, disseminated consciousness surpassing individual personality'. William Blake expresses something of Louis le Broquy's way of writing white icons:

> The vision of Christ which thou dost see
> Is my vision's greatest enemy ...
> Both read our Bibles day and night
> But thou read'st black where I read white.

9. Richard Kearney, *Navigations*, Lilliput, Dublin, 2006, pp301-305.

### OCTOBER: THREE MOVEMENTS OF BRIAN FRIEL

October of the twentieth century is represented by Brian Friel, who began his life, let us remember, on the road to priesthood. He left Maynooth after two years in the national seminary in the 1940s, where 'he explored the vocation which he believed he had for the priesthood.' He later said in 1972, when he was forty-three years of age: 'I hope that between now and my death I will have acquired a religion, a philosophy, a sense of life, that will make the end less frightening than it appears to me at this moment.'[10]

He was born in January 1929. Much of his life has been spent in the two adjuncts to the underground cathedral north and west of the millennium spire: the Abbey and the Gate Theatres. Celebrating the centenary of the founding of the Abbey Theatre, and discussing possibilities for its new location, forces us to examine the role of such theatre. In a poem written in 1932 called 'Three Movements', W. B. Yeats gives a parable of motivation for such space:

Shakespearean fish swam the sea, far away from land
Romantic fish swam in nets coming to the hand;
What are all those fish that lie gasping on the strand![11]

Classical fare and popular acclaim can determine the list of plays to be performed in our national theatres each year. Theatre can be entertainment or propaganda. The first is gauged by box-office success, the second remains the prerogative of those in charge. The founders of the original Abbey Theatre had higher ambitions than either of these quite legitimate variations. In his acceptance speech in Stockholm of the Nobel prize for literature in 1923, W. B. Yeats chose to speak of the Irish Dramatic Movement: 'I think as I speak these words of how deep down we have gone, below all that is individual, modern and restless, seeking foundations for an Ireland that can only come into existence in a Europe that is still but a dream.'[12] Excavating the deep structures of humanity and prompting an existence still only a dream was part of the business of a National Theatre.

10. Richard Pine, *Brian Friel and Ireland's Drama*, London, 1990, pp 17-18.
11. W. B. Yeats, *The Poems*, ed Daniel Albright, Everyman, p 290.
12. W. B. Yeats, *Autobiographies*, London, Macmillan, 1991, p 555.

From the beginning the Abbey Theatre was dogged by ambiguities of principle and purpose. As Tom Kettle suggested at the Irish Literary Society in 1906, two years after the Abbey made its appearance: nobody had done more than W. B. Yeats to create an Irish Theatre and nobody had done more than he to prevent anybody from going there![13] Although few critics would question Yeats's stature as one of the great lyric poets of the twentieth century, his reputation as playwright has often been questioned. Critics condemned his own plays as tediously esoteric and his taste in drama as minimalist if not obscurantist.

Trying to define what he meant by 'National literature' Yeats, although having 'no great love for definitions' goes on to 'define it in some such way as this:'

> It is the work of writers who are moulded by influences that are moulding their country, and who write out of so deep a life that they are accepted there in the end ... I mean by deep life that [writers] must put into their writing the emotions and experiences that have been most important to themselves.[14]

Playwrights of the calibre that Yeats would admire help us to achieve what Peter Brook has described as 'a genuine but fleeting experience of what could be a higher state of evolution.'[15] And theatre of this kind is capable of reaching the deepest levels of the unconscious. 'We shall do nothing' Yeats wrote to T. Sturge Moore on 4 October 1907, 'till we have created a criticism which will insist on the poet's right to educate his audience as a musical composer does his.' As the Polish Theatre Director, Jerzy Grotowski later suggested, this requires a ritualistic 'Holy Theatre' in which 'spectators and performers share a profoundly spiritual understanding of life.'[16]

The argument still goes on. In trying to establish some criteria

13. Quoted in Roy Foster, *W. B. Yeats, A Life*, Volume I: *The Apprentice Mage*, Oxford University Press, 1999, p 330.

14. W. B. Yeats, *Explorations*, London, Macmillan, 1962, pp 156-157.

15. Interview with A. C. Smith, Orghast at Persepolis, London, Eyre Methuen,1972, p 52, quoted in Flannery, op. cit. p 370.

16. cf James W. Flannery, *W. B. Yeats and the Idea of a Theatre*, Yale University Press, 1976, pp 368-9.

for the kind of drama and the kind of playwright which a National Theatre should perform and promote, a plea should be made for serious examination of some of 'those fish that lie gasping on the strand'.

Brian Friel is the kind of playwright Yeats was promoting. 'I would like to write a play that would capture the peculiar spiritual, and indeed material, flux that this country [Ireland] is in at the moment. This has got to be done, for me anyway ... at local level, and hopefully this will have meaning for people in other countries. The canvas can be as small as you wish, but the more accurately you write and the more truthful you are, the more validity your play will have for the world,'[17] Friel said in an interview in 1970. Since then he has written over twenty such plays. The four he wrote in the last decade before the new millennium suggest that he is trying to salvage a 'reality principle' which comes from 'so deep a life' that it must eventually 'find acceptance here' if we are to retain something of our 'real soul'.

The first of these plays of the nineties is *Dancing at Lughnasa* (1990). Even using the box-office criterion this was a dramatic success, playing to packed houses in Dublin, New York and London until eventually becoming a major Hollywood film. The play tells of a missionary priest sent home from Uganda because he has 'gone bush' or has been 'touched by the sun'. Instead of converting the 'pagans' to the religion he was sent out to preach, he is gradually being converted to their way of life, to their religion.

Home for him is Ballybeg, and the scene is the kitchen of the Mundy family, two miles outside the village. Ballybeg (*Baile Beag*, meaning small town in Irish, with the word *baile* also having the connotation 'home') is the setting for all four of these plays. It is a representative microcosm of contemporary Ireland.

The life of this family, five women on their own, is drearily mundane. And then something happens. They re-learn how to dance. The women of Ireland become empowered by the dance which reconnects them to 'being'. The stage instructions say that Irish dance music is heard on the radio.

Maggie turns round. Her head is cocked to the beat, to the

17. *The Irish Times*, 12 February 1970.

music. She is breathing deeply, rapidly. Now her features become animated by a look of defiance, of aggression; a crude
mask of happiness. For a few seconds she stands still, listening, absorbing the rhythm, surveying her sisters with her
defiant grimace. Now she spreads her fingers (which are cov-
ered with flour), pushes her hair back from her face, pulls her
hands down her cheeks and patterns her face with an instant
mask. At the same time she opens her mouth and emits a
wild raucous 'Yaaaah!' – and immediately begins to dance,
arms, legs, hair, long bootlaces flying.

The others join in. Eventually even Kate 'who has been
watching the scene with unease, with alarm, suddenly leaps to
her feet, flings her head back, and emits a loud 'Yaaaah!'

Kate dances alone, totally concentrated, totally private; a
movement that is simultaneously controlled and frantic; a
weave of complex steps that takes her quickly round the
kitchen, past her sisters, out to the garden, round the summer
seat, back to the kitchen; a pattern of action that is out of character and at the same time ominous of some deep and true
emotion.

All this is 'done' on stage. Friel is only prompting the scene
silently from behind. Like a rite or a spell. It is a retrieval of something 'traditional', something Celtic. The festival of Lughnasa is a
fertility rite at the beginning of the harvest. Even as late as 1962,
when Máire MacNeill published her definitive study, she found
that 'Lughnasa was celebrated until recently in ninety-five
heights and by ten lakes and five river banks'.[18]

The play ends with the following lines from Michael, the nar-
rator of the story:

When I remember it, I think of it as dancing. Dancing with
eyes half closed because to open them would break the spell.
Dancing as if language had surrendered to movement – as if
this ritual, this wordless ceremony, was now the way to
speak, to whisper private and sacred things, to be in touch
with some otherness. Dancing as if the very heart of life and

18. Máire MacNeill, *The Festival of Lughnasa*, Comhairle Bhéaloideas
Éireann, UCD, 1982.

all its hopes might be found in those assuaging notes and those hushed rhythms and in those silent and hypnotic movements. Dancing as if language no longer existed because words were no longer necessary ...[19]

This play touched some deep chord in audiences everywhere. It triggered an interest in Irish dancing which became chart-topping entertainment. The metaphysics got lost again in the market-place.

*Wonderful Tennessee* (1993), was not a box-office success. Here Friel had us back on the most god-forsaken pier in Donegal. The long lump of cement jutting out into the Atlantic was now Ballybeg, and we were sitting there 'killing time'. The cast, like ourselves, were waiting to be taken to 'a destination of wonder'. Here we are in Ballybeg waiting to travel across the sea to *Oileán Draíochta*, 'Island of otherness; Island of Mystery.'

When you are sitting on the last ditch in Europe, Samuel Beckett is reported to have said, explaining why there were so many artists in Ireland, there's nothing else to do but sing. The cast sing the whole night through and tell stories, because the ferryman never comes and they are left 'here' when they were meant to be going 'there'. And the singing and the stories are all to put down the hours, to kill time. One of the group who is dying of cancer plays the piano accordion. 'He plays all day long. As if he were afraid to stop.' The others join in the singing. 'A cheap song.' 'Boisterous singing, raucous singing, slightly tiddley, day-excursion singing,' the stage directions tell us. Song is certainly not existence here. There is no life 'here' so 'we're all going on a summer holiday.' And it is 'wonderful!' (the word is repeated over fifty times in the play): *Wonderful Tennessee*.[20] Our hope lies in America. 'That is the place / That shapes our destiny –' (sung to the air of *Abide with me*.) 'Next parish Boston, folks!'

'So, we're stuck here! We're going nowhere!' and 'waiting for anything makes you a bit edgy.' One of the group is writing a book on *The Measurement of Time and Its Effect on European Civilisation*. Being and Time! He goes for a walk and has a 'vision.'

19. Brian Friel, *Dancing at Lughnasa*, Faber, 1990, p 71.
20. Brian Friel, *Wonderful Tennessee*, Gallery Press, 1993.

'As if it had been waiting for a sign – suddenly a dolphin rose up out of the sea. And for thirty seconds, maybe a minute, it danced for me ... And for that thirty seconds ... it never once touched the water – was free of it – had nothing to do with water.'

And Brian Friel is trying to show us through this 'Ballybeg epiphany' that if we learnt how to dance really and truly, if we cherished our surroundings, if we dwelt here as if it were good for us to be here, if we had some ritualistic connection with our own earth, then 'maybe we could be put in *touch*'.

'In touch with what?' The answer of the playwright is 'Whatever it is we desire but can't express. What is beyond language. The inexpressible. The ineffable.' That is what the dance puts us in touch with because 'that's the only way it could be written, isn't it? A book without words!' The dolphin dances and is removed from its element. One of the characters in the play, Berna, jumps off the pier into the sea. Her watch stops: 'salt-water finished it.' She was out of her element. Dance is a different way of marking time, a way in which time gives access to 'being'.

*Molly Sweeney* (1994)[21] is a parable about Ireland. The main character is blind. Her husband and her doctor are anxious that she have an operation to recover her sight. She agrees to undergo the operation to please them. They are so enthusiastic about it she cannot bear to disappoint them. The operation is only partly successful. She moves from a situation in which she is totally blind to one in which she cannot see. There is a very slight 'improvement' which is a huge triumph at the medical level but which leaves Molly worse off than she was before the operation. She is then deserted by both the doctor and her husband, who lose interest in her once the exciting operation has been performed, and she ends her life in a sanatorium.

The climax to the first act is Molly's description of the wild horn-pipe she danced the night before Rice, the doctor, did the operation on her eyes. She is completely 'at home' in her own house, in space and time, as she 'weaves between all those people, darting between chairs and stools and cushions and bottles and glasses with complete assurance and absolute confidence.'

---

21. Brian Friel, *Molly Sweeney*, Gallery Press, 1994.

It is only when the music stops that she stumbles. Dancing is, for her, a way of understanding. The play is a parable about Ireland and 'the peculiar spiritual, indeed material, flux that this country is in at the moment'. It is a drama about 'vision' about how we 'know' and what we know, about 'seeing things'. It is about dancing to our own rhythm or agreeing to be operated on by our mentors, to adopt their way of seeing things, their vision. Frank, her husband, wants her to buy into an advertised world instead of dwelling accurately in her own. Molly ends up neither seeing nor being blind. She is in an in-between state where she can no longer remain at home but has to live out her days in an institution, getting rare visits from friends and rarer ones from her husband. 'Blindsight' is the important term for this limbo. Molly Sweeney is portrayed as victim of untrustworthy visionaries.

'We are no longer West Britains, we are East Americans', Friel has warned, and we are hardly capable of assessing all the exotic flotsam and jetsam that washes onto our shores. We import existence from our neighbours.

In 1997, on the brink of the new millennium, when Ireland was being hailed as EC wonderchild (Miracle Molly) and 'Europe's boom town' economically speaking, Friel paints quite a different picture in *Give Me Your Answer Do* (1997) at the Abbey. The play opens with a young woman, suffering from some acute depression, sitting up in bed, rigid, paralysed, speechless and autistic. The play closes with the same scene. And why? The play looks for a verdict. It asks the question of Daisy: Give me your answer do. Daisy is mother of the child. She has got to the point of being unable even to visit her daughter. The daughter cannot speak. She is depicted as offspring of a failed artist. Her grandfather is a waster, sharing his life between petty thieving and pilfering on the one hand, and jaunty song-and-dance routines on the other.

During the play, her father, the artist, is being tempted to sell his *corpus*, his artistic oeuvre, his complete works, to an American university archive which will set him up for life financially. There is a danger that the Americans won't buy. They have already bought the works of a fellow 'artist' who unashamedly writes for the popular market. The hero is tempted to include in the bargain offer of his own work, two 'pornographic' novels he wrote when his daughter first became ill.

What will be the verdict, Friel is asking Daisy, on our artistic heritage – part of which is, of course, the Abbey Theatre itself – on the prophetic vocation with which our artists were so richly endowed? Did they teach us how to dance or did they dance to the tune of the highest bidder?

Whatever the hope of keeping an Abbey Theatre alive for the next hundred years, it can only be worthwhile if this space itself holds open the possibility of access to a world quite other than the one we now inhabit. It should support Yeats's conviction, articulated by James W. Flannery: 'that religious experience and the ritualistic expression of that experience can provide the basis of profoundly significant theatre.'[22]

There are certain playwrights whose work, whether it be a recognised classic, or a box-office hit, should be performed and preserved by theatres somewhere in the country so that the possibility of imaginative evolution can be kept open. Otherwise our future is governed by market forces in the meretricious hands of politicians. Such plays are life-support machines, 'as if this ritual, this wordless ceremony, was now the way to speak, to whisper private and sacred things, to be in touch with some otherness.'[23]

22. James W. Flannery, *W. B. Yeats and the Idea of a Theatre*, Yale University Press, 1976, pp 372.
23. Brian Friel, *Dancing at Lugh*nasa, London, Faber, 1990, p 71.

SEPTEMBER: BLACKBIRD HUMMING IN THE DEAD OF NIGHT

September of the twentieth century is represented by Seamus Heaney who celebrated his seventieth birthday on 13 April 2009.

His twelfth collection of poems, *District and Circle*,[24] arrived to navigate the Underground Cathedral in 2006, forty years after his first: *Death of a Naturalist*. 'The Underground train journey which is the motif of the title sequence,' he tells Ben Napasstek in an interview for *The Times* in March 2006, 'really starts in 1962, when I had a holiday job in London and rode either the District or the Circle line every day.' Forty years later 'what's different is the level of awareness'. That level of awareness is not only heightened by his own ageing process but by 'the actuality of the bombings of the London Tube train in July 2005'.

Of course this is true, but there is more to it than the historico-political awareness ('History not to be granted the last word / Or the first claim' [56]). There is an ontological frisson also attached to the truth that 'an underground journey is shadowed with a certain menace'. This poetic journey is not just a sensitive twenty-first-century tourist trip, it is pioneering work on behalf of humanity. 'Ground gives ... nothing resettles right' [13]. Such dislocation is anthropological and not just topographical. 'The associations are' he admits to those who are searching for his / her [or their] usual themes, 'primarily with London rather than Ireland or the countryside, but on second thoughts a reader might realise, "Ah yes, in spite of the London poem, in most of the others, he's circling his own district".' After forty years a great deal has happened to expand the farmyard, to cause the 'naturalist' to die a thousand deaths. Remaining in your own district is a kind of death: 'A home-based man at home' finds himself 'in the end with little [69].' It is important to allow fresh air to circle the district even if only 'a CD of Bach is making the rounds / of the common or garden air [72].' So many aliens have invaded in the meantime:

---

24. Seamus Heaney, *District and Circle*, London, Faber and Faber, 2006. For the remainder of this section I shall refer to this work by page number in a square bracket.

Every time they landed in the district, there was an extraness in the air, as if a gate had been left open in the usual life, as if something might get in or get out [39].

'Circling his own district' for a poet is undertaking an archaeological dig on behalf of humanity. This is the underground transport system for a new metaphysics. Truth is here being unearthed by the most accomplished digger. Has he not received a Nobel prize for digging? 'Seamus, make me a side-arm to take on the earth/A suitable tool for digging and grubbing the ground' [25]. The danger of course has been the burden of expectation and the ambassadorial demands which such honours also confer. You could spend the rest of your life on parade with the shovel held aloft. Not so here. The opposite, in fact. Instead of being atrophied by the effects of the Nobel trophy he 'gathered/From the display-case peat my staying powers.' And 'once I felt the air/I was like turned turf in the breath of God ...' He maintained his humility, his earthiness. 'I want a hand-to-hand engagement with myself,' he explains, as much to himself as to the interviewer, 'self-forgetfulness rather than self-consciousness.' The result is freshly mined, original, unalloyed truth. Truth which has never before been articulated and which cannot be translated into political or psychological jargon. And this truth is also Heaney himself being dug up: 'a spade-plate slid and soughed and plied/At my buried ear, and the levered sod/Got lifted up.' The 'buried ear' is unearthed and primed to listen. This is the original meaning of humility, an ear fashioned from the earth [*humus* as the Latin word for earth].

Not the fervent mystical bond with nature which allowed the Romantic movement to see earth as a glossy surface with Wordsworth on his skates scoring sheet music several inches above the ground, 'As he flashed from the clutch of earth along its curve and left/it scored the whet and scud of steel on placid ice'[22]. Heaney does not skate some inches above the icy surface of the earth. He, like the ground hog, surfaces through the topsoil barely distinguishable from the mud, the dirt, the soil, from which he has been dredged. These poems are about where the human being stands in the cosmos, the human being who has recognised that we need to go underground to find roots.

'Cattle out in the rain, their knowledgeable/Solid standing and readiness to wait,/These I learned from' [57].

There is a whole underground continent which lay hidden to most citizens of the universe until discoveries were made at the beginning of the last century. Such discoveries require a new cartography and a metaphysics adjusted to the map of humanity unveiled. Hence the need for an underground map of District and Circle. The necessity to circle the district is finely expressed by the late Czeslaw Milosz quoted here in the fourth sonnet of 'The Tollund Man in Springtime': 'the soul exceeds its circumstances'. *Circumstare* could be the Latin for *District and Circle*. 'Not only do you have the archetype of the journey to the land of the dead' but beneath that again you have the abyss from whence such archetypes emerge. Philosophy to date has been an explanation of the universe and our position within it from the perspective of human consciousness. Revelations of an unconscious area underpinning this carefully mapped scenario spell its redundancy, its incapacity to cope with the real situation which pertains. New methods, new approaches are necessary. We are beginning to realise that this unconscious quagmire can be logged into by an art which lures us to the borders of impenetrability. Something akin to a psychic earthquake has occurred which has caused the dislocation of our centre of gravity:

> The centre of the total personality no longer coincides with the ego, but with a point midway between the conscious and the unconscious. This would be the point of a new equilibrium, a new centring of the total personality, a virtual centre which, on account of its focal position between conscious and unconscious ensures for the personality a new and more solid foundation.[25]

When a horse is required to perform the somewhat unnatural task of jumping a fence its centre of gravity moves into the area of its neck. This explains why jockeys lean forward over the horses' necks when jumping. A somewhat similar shift of metaphysics has been caused by recent acknowledgements about the

---

25. C. G. Jung, 'The Relations between the Ego and the Unconscious' *Collected Works*, Vol 7, Two Essays on Analytical Psychology (Bollingen Series XX, 1966) p 221.

fundamental shape of human being. The ground is moving and we are moving with it.

Hurtling 'through galleried earth,' as Heaney describes our voyage through such underground systems, standing up is as difficult as finding one's feet on an overcrowded tube train.

> Stepping on to it across the gap,
> On to the carriage metal, I reached to grab
> The stubby black roof-wort and take my stand.
> From planted ball of heel to heel of hand
> A sweet traction and heavy down-slump stayed me.

Such is the new 'stance' to be adopted to achieve alignment with the centre of gravity astride both worlds, '... then a long centrifugal/Haulage of speed through every dragging socket' [19]. The old stability of *terra firma* vanishes as we negotiate the swaying gangway. This marshy place, this bog, has been the focus of Heaney's poetic work and as John Burnside suggests: 'the original artist finds a source, a well spring, and spends a lifetime attuning himself to its dark, underground current.'[26] How do we achieve balance along this new centre of gravity? Heaney is his own Tollund man in springtime dragged up out of the bog. In a series of six sonnets he describes how 'on the sixth day' he, the Tollund Man, 'got lifted up' out of the bog 'brown and bare'. Almost as he the poet was lifted into the display case on the international stage by Nobel laureate status: 'the plain mysteriousness/of your sheeted self inside that neck-tied cope/ Half sleeveless surplice, half hoodless Ku Klux cape.' This last quotation is from a poem about having a haircut as a child in an elaborate swivel-chair of a barber's shop but the imagery contains temptation towards using such pedestals to become bishop, priest or sectarian murderer. The word 'cope' derives from the Latin *caput* meaning 'head,' the same root as 'cape' or 'cap'. The head has shifted to surround the whole body, a downward surge. But still such emblematic garments, such 'overalls' symbolise, in these images, priestly dignity and purity; 'surplice,' the second image, is an 'angelic' white garment used sometimes by choirs to give the effect of wings and derived from *super-*

---

26. *The Scotsman*, Saturday 1 April 2006.

*pellicium*, over one's *pellis* meaning 'skin.' It was probably simply a respectably clean item worn for worship over grubby clothes. We have to discard such angelic garb and wear an altogether more earthy 'helmet' and *superpellicium* to plumb the depths of contemporary shamanism.

Heaney is developing an alphabet of metaphysical archaeology and a vocabulary to help us adapt to 'being in depth': the call to be astride the abyss between conscious and unconscious awareness. In most languages, especially the romance languages, the copula which represents 'being' is linked with the notion of standing. The verb 'to be' came long after recognition that I am standing here and you are standing there:

> Bearings taken, markings, cardinal points,
> Options, obstinacies, dug heels and distance
> Here and there and now and then, a stance [12].

The Italian *stato* and the French *été* come from the Latin *stare* (to stand) as participles of the verbs *essere* and *être*. The same would be true for old Celtic. Being, as an ontological and philosophical concept is based upon the experience of stability and rest, a stance taken. 'The way you had to stand' [5], 'the shaft to be socketed in dead true and dead straight' [25], 'Spot-rooted' [18], 'on the spot,' [54], 'I take my stand in front of my house of life' [76]. 'Here's we're like sentries' [73]. He 'stood off,/ Bulrush, head in air, far from its lough' [25]. These poems are there like standing stones 'after the fire' [16] 'to make them realise what had stood so.'

Becoming, on the other hand, is based upon the perception of motion, of coming and going: *devenir, diventare, divenire* mean to become in three such languages, whereas the German word *werden* is linked with the Latin *vertere* meaning to turn. Language, like poetry, surprises these realities in their primary ontological emergence and finds the words to usher them into consciousness. Later they are circumscribed with a whole vocabulary of technical metaphysics. District, in this collection, is your place of rest. It comes from the Latin *distringere* which means delineating or marking off. It describes a territory divided or defined for whatever purposes, usually a jurisdiction for administration. Circle adds the movement, the 'corona of gold' [65].

The human stance has to be versatile and sturdy, 'any for-wardness was unwelcome and bodies blindsided to themselves and other bodies' [18].

> The way you had to stand to swing the sledge
> Your two knees locked, your lower back shock-fast
> As shields in a testudo, spine and waist
> A pivot for the tight-braced, tilting rib-cage [5].

Each of us is responsible for our own posture in this shifting world. We can be given a totally wrong-headed version of what the world is like which will skew our position, falsify our an-thropological alignment. We have to follow with sensitivity and attention the orthodoxy of humanity 'keeping an eye/On the eye in the level/Before the cement set' [8].

You also have to stand up for yourself. On the other hand, 'if art teaches us anything' he says, trumping life/with a quote, 'it's that the human condition is private.' Privacy is essential to sur-vival, especially in the display-case. So that 'wherever the world was, we were somewhere else' [11]. But such privacy demands relationship and intimacy also, otherwise words turn to 'ice blocks.' 'If self is a location, so is love' [12]. Being as an under-grounded person requires a delicate blend of intimacy. It is easy to damage this with 'a Hagging Match' [62] or a 'planetary stand-off' [54] and yet it is necessary for each partner to stand their ground so that 'nothing gives on the rug or the ground be-neath it'[61], which means that 'when we moved I had your measure and you had mine.' Both have to be (in Rilke's words) 'guardians of each other's solitude.' 'Reticence'[42] is essential, 'keeping us together when together' [42]. And the poet wonders whether he succeeded in maintaining his side of the essential equation: 'There was never a scene/When I had it out with my-self or with another,/The loss occurred off-stage' [47]. And this was cowardice because the battleground should be on-stage, on the ontological patch that needs defending, 'each last tug and lap' [28]. His failure was caused by fear. He 'feared its coldness' [53], 'the coldness off her/Like the coldness off you' [58], the 'dawn stone-circle chill' [54]. And yet she played her part in 'Her open and closed relations with earth's work' [66].

But for her part, in response, only the slightest
Back-stiffening and standing of her ground
As her hand reached down and tightened around mine [12].

If there is fault, betrayal of position, of the necessary tension
between intimacy and privacy, it is his, committed out of cowardice and fear of the cold. 'And feared its coldness that still
seemed enough to iceblock ... every warm, mouthwatering
word of mouth' [53]. He should have stood his own ground to
accomplish earth's work and not to give into 'what conspired on
the spot to addle/Matter' [54]. The appropriate stance between
privacy and intimacy, the new centre of gravity for human
being, requires us:

To walk up to the bib
Upstream, in the give and take
Of her deepest, draggiest purchase
Countering, parting,

Getting back at her, sourcing
Her and your plashy self
Neither of you
Ready to let up [59].

There are times when we have to hurt one another ['carefully
manhandled'] to maintain the necessary equilibrium 'tilting and
hoisting, the one on the lower step/Bearing the brunt ... Not
averting eyes from her hurting bulk' [67]. It is a question of remaining 'absolute' of accomplishing absolution. *Solvere* means
to loose, and we are letting go of each other gradually [step by
step] to allow the essential privacy to establish itself as fruit of
the intimacy. And all of this is preparation for the final separation through intimacy which is our goal:

In the knowledge that no matter how above
Measure or expectation, all must be
Harvested and yielded, when a long life willingly
Cleaves to what's willed and grows in mute resolve [68].

Blackbird at the end sings the meaning of the song of love,
'You/whom I cleave to, hew to' [62]

Hedge-hop, I am absolute
For you, your ready talkback,
Your each stand-offish comeback

Such toing and froing is the prelude to alternative existence beyond our present circumstances. 'Call it the flight of the soul or the spirit. It helped me to lose my shyness of the vocabulary of eternity,' Heaney says in another interview about these poems:

On the grass when I arrive,
In the ivy when I leave.

It's you, blackbird, I love.

At the end of forty days, we are told in the Book of Genesis, Noah opened the porthole of the ark and released a blackbird to see if there was solid ground on which to land. Black on black is the Holy Spirit humming in the night.

# Acknowledgements

First and foremost I acknowledge the Holy Spirit as commissioner of this work, although the many shortcomings, the lack of imagination and understanding, are mine. After some years spent at the beginning of this century looking for the signs of the Holy Spirit's intervention in our world, I was led to the following conclusion on 12 November 2002: 'Glenstal Abbey must become the hub, the centre of a very much wider circle, a virtual community, whether connected as separate entities in other organisms, or incorporated in houses around the property is not yet clear, but they will be part of the constellation.'

Monasteries should be dwelling-places, with listening ears for the world around, essential parts of any society, providing touchstones for our deeper selves, for nature, for God. *Ausculta*, the Latin word for 'Listen,' is the first word in the Rule of Benedict. Monasteries should act as beehives of the invisible, making honey which can be tasted, out of otherwise unavailable nectar hidden in flowers designed to conceal it. Monasteries are breweries distilling wisdom from many sources, searching out new perspectives: ways of hearing, seeing, touching invisible life at every level.

> Glenstal would become like Clonmacnoise in Seamus Heaney's poem, a place where the abbot and the community help the artist to anchor the altar. The monastery becomes a place where artists can hope to tie whatever kite they happen to be flying to a firm and stable anchor. The monastery as silent hub of that fireworks display which art and culture need to scatter with reckless flamboyancy into the night.'[1]

1. Mark Patrick Hederman, *Walkabout, Life as Holy Spirit*, Columba, Dublin, 2005.

Since those words were written and published in 2005, in a quite unanticipated move of the Holy Spirit I was elected Abbot of Glenstal at the end of October 2008. Christopher Dillon, my predecessor, said wryly: 'You have been speaking so much about the Holy Spirit recently, now the bird has come home to roost!' I understood this happening to be undiluted working of the Holy Spirit and the charge to put in place whatever the same Holy Spirit might suggest.

In the meantime, I acknowledge all the secret agents who supplied the wherewithal to write this book. I have already acknowledged connection and correspondence with Lorcan Walshe, Brendan Kennelly, Seamus and Marie Heaney in the previous book already mentioned. Ciarán Forbes has persecuted me over the years with books and quotations from John McGahern. He also gave me a copy of McGahern's essays which became a guidebook to the Underground Cathedral.

Louis le Brocquy asked me to open his exhibition at the Fenton Gallery on the eve of his 90th birthday on 10 November 2006. His wife, Anne Madden, invited me to the opening of her retrospective exhibition at IMMA on 26 June 2007. At this opening I was seated at the same table as Tom Murphy and Jane Brennan. Jane said I must come to see her b*spoke Theatre production of *Honour* by Joanna Murray-Smith at the Samuel Beckett Theatre in Trinity College. I said I never went anywhere unless I received three signs that I should do so. She said she could organise that. I went on Friday 13 July 2007. The first person I met going into the foyer was Patrick Mason. His interpretation of Tom Murphy's *The Gigli Concert* became normative. Later Jane Brennan asked me to write a programme note for her b*spoke Theatre production of *The Sanctuary Lamp* directed by Tom Murphy himself in July 2008. I saw at Glór Theatre, Ennis, in December 2009, the last performance on the Irish Tour of Garry Hynes' and The Druid's production of *The Gigli Concert*, with Derbhle Crotty, Denis Conway and Peter Sullivan.

My friend Ben Kelly asked me to preside over his marriage in March 2008. Was I surprised to discover that his bride was Justine Mitchell, who was playing Olga in Brian Friel's version of *Three Sisters* by Chekhov from 18 June (my birthday) to 2 August 2008, and later Hedda Gabler in Friel's version of Ibsen's masterpiece, which opened at The Gate Theatre in September 2008, the year before Friel celebrated his 80th birthday? Nor was I surprised to be again at The Gate Theatre with Sacha Abercorn for their acclaimed production of Friel's tour de force for the Underground Cathedral, *The Faith Healer*, on the auspicious evening of 09/09/09. Such coincidences are the way in which the Holy Spirit forces my attention and guides my steps.

Michael D. Higgins arrived at Glenstal in February 2009, with the poem which opens this book. Andy O'Mahony and Bernadette Madden sent me Peggy O'Brien's book, *Writing Lough Derg*, to review for their RTÉ Radio programme *Off the Shelf*. Later I had stimulating correspondence with the author. Caroline Walsh of the *Irish Times* sent me Susan Gubar's book on Judas to review. Otherwise I would not have known of the existence of these books which form important pieces of the jig-saw here.

I saw *Woman and Scarecrow* at the Peacock Theatre and two weeks later attended the pre-performance discussion of the play on Tuesday 30 October 2007, hosted by Selina Cartmell, who had directed the play. Many in the audience expressed their feelings that this play was for them the life of Christ with a woman acting as Jesus. There was one day only when I could see both *The Great Blue Hand* at the Ark in Temple Bar and *Marble* at The Abbey but the first was booked out. I wrote to Marina Carr and she happened to be in Dublin teaching on 6 March 2009. So, she accompanied me into the Ark. At a symposium organised by Professor Michael Conway in Maynooth on Transcendence and the Arts, in May 2009, I met Selina Cartmell, in conversation with Liam Tracey OSM discussing 'Staging the Beyond'. My contribution to that symposium was an early version of this book, since published in *The Irish Theological Quarterly*.

Finally, my thanks to Fanny Howe, Glenstal's poet in residence, and to my confrères Michael O'Connor, who keeps me in touch with everything, Basil Forde, who supplied copies of *The Irish Rosary* from 1907, Simon Sleeman and Martin Browne who helped me to put some shape on this text.